A Paines Plough and Theatre Royal Plymouth
production

T0341944

YOU STUPID
DARKNESS!

by Sam Steiner

The first performance of *You Stupid Darkness!* took place on
7 February 2019 at Theatre Royal Plymouth.

You Stupid Darkness! transferred to
Southwark Playhouse, London, in January 2020.

Supported using public funding by
**ARTS COUNCIL
ENGLAND**

You Stupid Darkness!

by Sam Steiner

Cast

FRANCES	Jenni Maitland
JON	Andy Rush
ANGIE	Lydia Larson
JOEY	Andrew Finnigan

Production Team

Direction	James Grieve
Design	Amy Jane Cook
Lighting	Peter Small
Sound	Dominic Kennedy
Associate Designer	Grace Venning
Movement	Annie-Lunnette Deakin-Foster
Director on placement	Jonathan Bensusan Bash
Producer	Kitty Wordsworth
Associate Producer	Bellaray Bertrand-Webb
Company Stage Manager on book	Carrie Hitchman
Assistant Stage Manager	Rosie Morgan
Production Manager	Colin Everitt
Costume Supervisor	Rosie Whiting
Production Electrician	Douglas Finlay
LX Programmer	Tom Davis
Marketing Consultants	Target Live

With thanks to White Light Ltd, GLP and PRAX.

SAM STEINER (Writer)

Sam is a playwright and screenwriter from Manchester. His debut play, the award-winning LEMONS LEMONS LEMONS LEMONS LEMONS, was first produced by Walrus Theatre (a company he co-founded), and has subsequently been performed all over the world, in eight different languages. Since then Sam's work on stage has included YOU STUPID DARKNESS! (Paines Plough/Theatre Royal Plymouth); KANYE THE FIRST (HighTide); and most recently A TABLE TENNIS PLAY (Walrus Theatre) at the Edinburgh Fringe. Other pieces of Sam's work have been showcased at the Royal Exchange, Soho, Southwark Playhouse, Sala Beckett in Barcelona, and the Cannes and London Film Festivals. He completed an attachment at Paines Plough as its Playwright Fellow and holds an MA in Screenwriting from the National Film and Television School. Sam is currently under commission at Paines Plough and the Almeida, and is developing a television project with Euston North, and a film project with Sunny March.

JENNI MAITLAND (Frances)

Jenni's theatre credits include: EMILIA (Vaudeville/West End/Shakespeare's Globe); BY JEEVES (Landor); GUYS AND DOLLS (Cambridge Arts Theatre); THE RIVALS (Southwark Playhouse); A LITTLE NECK (Goat and Monkey); IS EVERYTHING OK? (nabokov); HOBSON'S CHOICE (Chichester Festival Theatre/UK tour); A CHORUS OF DISAPPROVAL (The Mill At Sonning); NORTHANGER ABBEY (York Theatre Royal/Salisbury Playhouse/UK tour); IN EXTREMIS (Shakespeare's Globe); CORAM BOY (National Theatre); KING LEAR (Creation Theatre Company); PLASTIC JESUS (Old Vic); HOUSE AND GARDEN, FEN, SHARP RELIEF (Salisbury Playhouse); AMADEUS (York Theatre Royal); BLITHE SPIRIT (Derby Playhouse) and DAISY PULLS IT OFF (Lyric, West End).

Television includes: THERE SHE GOES, DOCTORS and EASTENDERS (BBC).

ANDY RUSH (Jon)

Andy's theatre credits include: THE HERE AND THIS AND NOW (Southwark Playhouse/Theatre Royal Plymouth); I GOT SUPERPOWERS FOR MY BIRTHDAY (Paines Plough/Half Moon Production); LOVE, LIES, AND TAXIDERMY (Paines Plough/Clwyd Theatr Cymru/Sherman Cymru); GROWTH (Paines Plough); TIPPING THE VELVET, DICK WHITTINGTON AND HIS CAT (Lyric Hammersmith); UNIDENTIFIED ITEM IN THE BAGGING AREA (Old Red Lion); JUMPERS FOR GOALPOSTS (Paines Plough); HELLO GOODBYE (Hampstead); THE KITCHEN SINK (Bush); SENSE (Hen & Chicken); ANNA KARENINA (Arcola); TWELFTH NIGHT (The Lamb Players); ROMEO AND JULIET (Everyman).

Recent television credits include: TOMMY COOPER: NOT LIKE THAT, LIKE THIS (ITV); NEW TRICKS (Wall To Wall); WIZARDS Vs ALIENS, CASUALTY, HOLBY CITY and WATERLOO ROAD (BBC). Recent film credits include: ID2: SHADWELL ARMY (Universal Pictures) and HERE AND NOW (Wrapt Films).

LYDIA LARSON (Angie)

Lydia's theatre credits include: FINDING FASSBENDER (Pleasance, Edinburgh); SKIN A CAT (UK tour/Bunker/Vault; Offie shortlisted: Best Actress), BRUTAL CESSATION (Assembly); WE HAVE FALLEN (Underbelly); THE AFTER-DINNER JOKE and SPRINGS ETERNAL (Orange Tree); PERSUASION (Salisbury Playhouse); PRIDE AND PREJUDICE (Theatre Royal Bath/UK tour); 24 HOUR PLAYS (Old Vic); ARCADIA (SFP).

TV credits include: ROUTES (Channel 4); KIDNAPPED (Virgin) and DOCTORS (BBC). Film includes: A GIFT FROM BOB.

ANDREW FINNIGAN (Joey)

Andrew trained with The Customs House, South Shields.

Credits include: THE FIFTEEN STREETS (The Customs House, South Shields); BROKEN BISCUITS (Live/Paines Plough/UK tour); DRIP (Hull City of Culture/Boundless/tour) and GREAT NORTH RUN for BBC Radio 4.

Other credits include: THE RIVER and commercials for M&S and Oatibix.

JAMES GRIEVE (Direction)

James was Joint Artistic Director of Paines Plough 2010–2019. He was formerly co-founder and Artistic Director of nabokov and Associate Director at the Bush Theatre. His forthcoming work includes the world premiere of Alan Harris's FOR THE GRACE OF YOU GO I at Theatr Clwyd and a new production of CABARET for Gothenburg Opera in Sweden.

James's directing credits for Paines Plough include POP MUSIC by Anna Jordan; OUT OF LOVE by Elinor Cook; BLACK MOUNTAIN by Brad Birch; HOW TO BE A KID by Sarah McDonald-Hughes; THE ANGRY BRIGADE by James Graham; BROKEN BISCUITS and JUMPERS FOR GOALPOSTS by Tom Wells; HOPELESSLY DEVOTED and WASTED by Kate Tempest; AN INTERVENTION and LOVE, LOVE, LOVE by Mike Bartlett; FLY ME TO THE MOON by Marie Jones; TINY VOLCANOES by Laurence Wilson; YOU CANNOT GO FORWARD FROM WHERE YOU ARE RIGHT NOW by David Watson; THE SOUND OF HEAVY RAIN by Penelope Skinner and HAPPINESS by Nick Payne for BBC Radio 3.

Further credits include GOD'S DICE by David Baddiel (Soho); the new musical THE ASSASSINATION OF KATIE HOPKINS (Theatr Clwyd – winner Best Musical Production, UK Theatre Awards 2018); LES MISÉRABLES for Wermland Opera in Karlstad, Sweden; TRANSLATIONS (Sheffield Theatres/ ETT/Rose – winner Best Production, UK Theatre Awards 2014); 66 BOOKS: A NOBODY by Laura Dockrill; THE WHISKY TASTER by James Graham; ST PETERSBURG by Declan Feenan and PSYCHOGEOGRAPHY by Lucy Kirkwood (Bush); ARTEFACTS by Mike Bartlett (nabokov/Bush/national tour/Off-Broadway).

AMY JANE COOK (Design)

Amy Jane won the Wales Theatre Award for Best Design in 2017 for CONSTELLATION STREET at The Other Room. She was nominated for three Off West End Best Set Design Awards in 2018 for JELLYFISH (Bush); THE FUNERAL DIRECTOR (Southwark Playhouse) and NOT TALKING (Arcola).

Theatre credits include: JELLYFISH (National Theatre/Bush); THE SEASON (Royal & Derngate); THE IMPORTANCE OF BEING EARNEST (Watermill); YOU STUPID DARKNESS! (Plymouth Drum/Paines Plough); THE FUNERAL DIRECTOR (Southwark Playhouse/UK tour); ABSURD PERSON SINGULAR (Watford Palace Theatre); WAVE ME GOODBYE, THE RISE AND FALL OF LITTLE VOICE, INSIGNIFICANCE, ST NICHOLAS (Theatr Clwyd); NOT TALKING (Arcola); THOR & LOKI (Edinburgh/Assembly); LAVA (Nottingham Playhouse/UK tour); OUR BLUE HEAVEN (New Wolsey); UP 'N' UNDER (New Wolsey/UK tour/Fingersmiths); TO DREAM AGAIN (Theatr Clwyd/Polka); INSIGNIFICANCE (The Langham, NYC); THE 8TH (Barbican); MUDLARKS (Bush/ HighTide Festival); MEDEA, W11 (The Gate); 65 MILES, ONCE UPON A TIME IN WIGAN (Hull Truck); HAMLET (Young Vic/Maria Theatre); 66 BOOKS (Bush/Westminster Abbey); FLOODED GRAVE, WHERE'S MY SEAT? (Bush); CONSTELLATION STREET, THE INSOMNIA SEASON (The Other Room); MYDIDAE (Soho/Trafalgar Studios); GLORY DAZED (Soho); THE GIANT JAM SANDWICH (Derby Live/Polka). www.amyjanecook.com

PETER SMALL (Lighting)

Peter is an Offie and Theatre & Technology Award nominated lighting designer working across theatre, dance and opera.

Recent credits include BABY REINDEER (Bush/Edinburgh Fringe); SPIDERFLY (Theatre503); SQUARE GO (UK tour/59E59 Theater New York/Edinburgh Fringe); LIT (Clapham Omnibus/HighTide Aldeburgh Festival/Nottingham Playhouse); ANGRY ALAN (Soho/Aspen Fringe); as three of the 2019 Paines Plough Roundabout tour shows, DAUGHTERHOOD, DEXTER AND WINTER'S DETECTIVE AGENCY and ON THE OTHER HAND, WE'RE HAPPY; DO OUR BEST (Edinburgh Fringe); RADIO (Arcola); AD LIBIDO (Soho/VAULT Festival/Edinburgh Fringe); YOU STUPID DARKNESS! (Theatre Royal Plymouth); Paines Plough Roundabout Tour productions 2017–19, including the Offie-nominated BLACK MOUNTAIN; A GIRL IN SCHOOL UNIFORM (WALKS INTO A BAR) (Offie and Theatre & Technology Award Nominated – New Diorama) and ALL OR NOTHING (West End/tour).

Upcoming projects include productions with New Diorama and Paines Plough, among others.

DOMINIC KENNEDY (Sound)

Dominic is a sound designer and music producer for performance and live events; he has a keen interest in developing new work and implementing sound and music at an early stage in a creative process. Dominic is a graduate from Royal Central School of Speech and Drama. He has developed specialist skills in collaborative and devised theatre making, music composition and installation practices. His work often fuses found sound, field recordings, music composition and synthesis.

Recent design credits include: GOD'S DICE (Soho); A HISTORY OF WATER IN THE MIDDLE EAST (Royal Court); LIT

(Nottingham Playhouse); ROUNDABOUT SEASON 2019 (Paines Plough); YOU STUPID DARKNESS! (Paines Plough/Theatre Royal Plymouth); POP MUSIC (Paines Plough/Birmingham REP/Latitude); SKATE HARD TURN LEFT (Battersea Arts Centre); ROUNDABOUT SEASON 2018 (Paines Plough/Theatr Clwyd); ANGRY ALAN (Soho); THE ASSASSINATION OF KATIE HOPKINS (Theatr Clwyd); WITH A LITTLE BIT OF LUCK (Paines Plough/BBC Radio 1Xtra); RAMONA TELLS JIM (Bush); AND THE REST OF ME FLOATS (Outbox); I AM A TREE (Jamie Wood); BOX CLEVER (nabokov).

GRACE VENNING (Associate Designer)

Grace is a performance designer from London. She was a resident design assistant at the National Theatre from 2018–2019. In 2019 she was a finalist for the JMK Award with Jocelyn Cox, and for the inaugural Naomi Wilkinson Award for Stage Design with Told by an Idiot. She trained at the Royal Welsh College of Music and Drama.

Design credits include: IF NOT NOW, WHEN (National Theatre: Dorfman), BEFORE I WAS A BEAR; I WILL STILL BE WHOLE (WHEN YOU RIP ME IN HALF); FCUK'D (Bunker); TIME OF LISTENING (Snape Maltings); OPERA SCENES (Guildhall School of Music and Drama); LA BOHÈME (Clonter Opera); SEMELE (Mid Wales Opera tour); THE DEATH OF IVAN ILYICH (Attic Theatre Co.); STOP GIVING ME GRIEF (From the Forest Festival); MASTI MAJA (Sansaar Theatre Co.); THE COSMONAUT'S LAST MESSAGE TO THE WOMAN HE ONCE LOVED IN THE FORMER SOVIET UNION; ROAD (Bute Theatre, RWCMD).

ANNIE-LUNNETTE DEAKIN-FOSTER (Movement)

Annie-Lunnette is a passionate contemporary dance theatre choreographer, maker and movement director, and was a founding member of award-winning company, C-12 Dance Theatre.

Theatre credits: THE LAST NOËL by Chris Bush dir. by Jonathan Humphries, PAVILION by Emily White dir. by Tamara Harvey at Theatr Clwyd; CHIAROSCURO by Jackie Kay dir. by Lynette Linton at the Bush; ON THE OTHER HAND WE'RE HAPPY by Daf James, DAUGHTERHOOD by

Charley Miles and DEXTER AND WINTER'S DETECTIVE AGENCY by Nathan Byron dir. by Stef O'Driscoll for Roundabout; AESOP'S FABLES by Justin Audibert and Rachel Bagshaw at the Unicorn Theatre. www.annielunnettedeakinfoster.com.

KITTY WORDSWORTH (Producer)

Kitty is a freelance theatre, comedy and screen producer. She is executive producer and co-founder of Damsel Productions. Recent theatre and comedy producer credits include: SIBLINGS (Soho); THE AMBER TRAP (Theatre503); FABRIC (Soho/London tour); GROTTY, DAMSEL DEVELOPS (Bunker); FURY (Soho); DRY LAND (Jermyn Street); UNCENSORED (Theatre Royal Haymarket); TABS (workshop, Tristan Bates); A PORTOBELLO CHRISTMAS CAROL, SNOW WHITE AND THE SEVEN RUNAWAYS, THE NAIVETY: A JOURNEY, DICK WHIT, THE SNOW QUEEN, PETER PANTO (Tabernacle); BRUTE (Soho) and JULIET COWAN: EAT, PRAY, CALL THE POLICE (Live@Zedel). Associate theatre producer credits include: WHAT GIRLS ARE MADE OF (Soho) and A LEVEL PLAYING FIELD (Jermyn Street). She currently has productions in development including SOHO 6, a co-commission with Soho Theatre, and new musical LILITH, both with Damsel Productions. She also works part-time at West End production company, Lee Menzies Ltd, and in the marketing team at Ronnie Scott's Jazz Club. Coming up: MUM (The Playground Theatre) and BIN JUICE (Vaults).

Film producer credits include: LITTLE HARD (dir. Bel Powley and Alice Felgate); THE LAST BIRTHDAY (dir. Jaclyn Bethany); SUNDAY (dir. Daisy Stenham); ONCE UPON A TIME'S UP (dir. Denna Cartamkhoob).

CARRIE HITCHMAN (Company Stage Manager on book)

Carrie is a theatre maker, production/tour/stage manager who graduated from Rose Bruford in 2015. A few of her credits include: TYPICAL, DRAG BECOMES HER, THE GINGER SNAPPED, JINKX MONSOON – THE VAUDEVILLIANS, FREE ADMISSION – URSULA MARTINEZ, WILD BORE, VIR DAS: THE BOARDING DAS WORLD TOUR (Soho); POP MUSIC (Paines Plough); TRANSLUNAR PARADISE (Ad Infinitum); J STAGING A REVOLUTION (Belarus Free Theatre).

ROSIE MORGAN (Assistant Stage Manager)

Rosie is an Assistant Stage Manager who graduated from Bath Spa University in 2018. Some of her credits include: ALADDIN, SNOW WHITE AND THE SEVEN DWARFS (Malvern Theatres); DIE ZAUBERFLÖTE (Royal Academy of Music); TORCH SONG (The Turbine); GEORGIANA, LUCIO PAPIRIO DITTATORE (Buxton Opera House); AMOUR (Charing Cross); NANJING (Royal Exchange/Birmingham Rep); YOU STUPID DARKNESS! (Theatre Royal Plymouth); SEMITES (Bunker, Loco Klub); A FUNNY THING HAPPENED… (Finborough).

From the original performance at Theatre Royal Plymouth

Original Cast

FRANCES	Becci Gemmell
JON	David Carlyle
ANGIE	Lydia Larson
JOEY	Andrew Finnigan

Original Production Team

Direction	James Grieve
Design	Amy Jane Cook
Lighting	Peter Small
Sound	Dominic Kennedy
Movement	Annie-Lunnette Deakin-Foster
Assistant Director	Freddie Crossley
Line Producer	Hanna Streeter
Producer for Theatre Royal Plymouth	Louise Schumann
Company Stage Manager on book	Carrie Hitchman
Assistant Stage Manager	Rosie Morgan
Production Manager	Nick Soper
Costume Supervisor	Delia Lancaster
Head of Sound	Dan Mitcham
Drum Technician	Matt Hoyle

PAINES PLOUGH

Paines Plough tours the best new theatre to all four corners of the UK and around the world. Whether you're in Liverpool or Lyme Regis, Brighton or Berwick-Upon-Tweed, a Paines Plough show is coming to a theatre near you soon.

'The lifeblood of the UK's theatre ecosystem' *Guardian*

Paines Plough was formed in 1974 over a pint of Paines Bitter in the Plough pub. Since then we've produced more than 150 new productions by world-renowned playwrights like Stephen Jeffreys, Abi Morgan, Sarah Kane, Mark Ravenhill, Dennis Kelly, Mike Bartlett, Kate Tempest and Vinay Patel. We've toured those plays to hundreds of places from Bristol to Belfast to Brisbane.

'That noble company Paines Plough, de facto national theatre of new writing' *Daily Telegraph*

In the past three years we've produced 30 shows and performed them in more than 200 places across four continents. We tour to more than 30,000 people a year from Cornwall to the Orkney Islands; in village halls and Off-Broadway, at music festivals and student unions, online and on radio, and in our own pop-up theatre, Roundabout.

Our Programme 2020 premieres the best new British plays touring the length and breadth of the UK in theatres, clubs and pubs everywhere from city centres to seaside towns. Roundabout hosts a jam-packed Edinburgh Festival Fringe programme and brings mini-festivals to each stop on its nationwide tour.

Our *Come To Where I'm From* app features 180 short audio plays available to download free from the App Store and GooglePlay.

'I think some theatre just saved my life' @kate_clement on Twitter

Paines Plough

Paines Plough Limited is a company limited by guarantee and a registered charity.
Registered Company no: 1165130
Registered Charity no: 267523

Paines Plough, 4th Floor, 43 Aldwych, London WC2B 4DN
+ 44 (0) 20 7240 4533
office@painesplough.com
www.painesplough.com

 Follow @PainesPlough on Twitter

 Like Paines Plough at facebook.com/PainesPloughHQ

 Follow @painesplough on Instagram

Donate to Paines Plough at justgiving.com/PainesPlough

Theatre
Royal
Plymouth

Theatre Royal Plymouth is a registered charity providing art, education and community engagement throughout Plymouth and the wider region. We engage and inspire many communities through performing arts and we aim to touch the lives and interests of people from all backgrounds. We do this by creating and presenting a breadth of shows on a range of scales, with our extensive creative engagement programmes, by embracing the vitality of new talent and supporting emerging and established artists, and by collaborating with a range of partners to provide dynamic cultural leadership for the city of Plymouth.

Recent productions and co-productions include THE UNRETURNING by Anna Jordan (with Frantic Assembly), ONE UNDER by Winsome Pinnock (with Graeae) and UNSUNG by Valentijn Dhaenens (with SkaGen and KVS, Richard Jordan Productions in association with Big in Belgium & Summerhall) and forthcoming productions include I THINK WE ARE ALONE by Sally Abbott (with Frantic Assembly), THE ROOMMATE by Jen Silverman and THIS LAND – a major large-scale production for the Mayflower400 commemorations directed by Alan Lane and performed by citizens of Plymouth UK and members of the Wampanoag tribe from Massachusetts USA.

TRP has a strong track record of presenting and producing international work from companies and artists including Ontroerend Goed, Big In Belgium at the Edinburgh Festival Fringe, Robert Lepage and the late Yukio Ninagawa. In March 2019 TRP unveiled Messenger, the UK's largest bronze sculpture created by the artist Joseph Hillier.

'Southwark Playhouse churn out arresting productions at a rate of knots'
Time Out

Southwark Playhouse is all about telling stories and inspiring the next generation of storytellers and theatre makers. It aims to facilitate the work of new and emerging theatre practitioners from early in their creative lives to the start of their professional careers.

Through our schools work we aim to introduce local people at a young age to the possibilities of great drama and the benefits of using theatre skills to facilitate learning. Each year we engage with more than 5,000 school pupils through free schools performances and long-term in school curriculum support.

Through our participation programmes we aim to work with all members of our local community in a wide-ranging array of creative drama projects that aim to promote cohesion, build confidence and encourage a lifelong appreciation of theatre.

Our theatre programme aims to facilitate and showcase the work of some of the UK's best up and coming talent with a focus on reinterpreting classic plays and up-and-coming plays of note. Our two atmospheric theatre spaces enable us to offer theatre artists and companies the opportunity to present their first fully realised productions. Over the past 25 years we have produced and presented early productions by many aspiring theatre practitioners, many of whom are now enjoying flourishing careers.

'A brand as quirky as it is classy' *The Stage*

For more information about our forthcoming season and to book tickets visit www.southwarkplayhouse.co.uk.

You can also support us online by joining our Facebook and Twitter pages.

Southwark Playhouse

YOU STUPID DARKNESS!

Sam Steiner

For everyone at Paines Plough

Thanks

Huge thanks to everyone I spoke to at Childline and Samaritans – David Dunne, Laura Clayson and Caroline Steiner in particular – for their time and insight.

To Marek Horn, Simon Stephens, Katherine Soper, Ed Madden and Charlotte Holtum for their perceptive notes.

To our cast, creative team and the staff at Theatre Royal Plymouth who have brought the script to life with such overwhelming imagination and detail.

To Simon Stokes for his inspiration, wisdom and confidence. It's a privilege to be a small part of his new writing legacy at TRP.

Most of all to James Grieve for his quiet, resonant provocations and for directing the play with such sensitivity and craft.

S.S.

Characters

FRANCES, *thirty-nine, heavily pregnant*
JON, *thirty-two*
ANGIE, *twenty-seven*
JOEY, *seventeen*

All of the scenes take place in the early hours of Wednesday mornings, between 12 a.m. and 4 a.m.

Note on Text

Because there is often a character taking a phone call, I have written the play in landscape with different columns for stuff that's going on at the same time. I've tried to put the most important stuff – the stuff that should be brought to the fore in production – in the left-hand column. Sometimes people end up talking between columns because they're halfway through a phone call or something.

A forward slash (/) indicates the point of interruption in overlapping dialogue.

An en-dash (–) indicates an interruption of speech or train of thought.

Ellipses (…) indicate either a trailing off, a breather or a hesitation.

Punctuation or lack thereof is written to suggest delivery rather than to conform to the rules of grammar.

An asterisk (*) indicates a time jump.

Set

A shabby-looking office. There are four or five desks facing the audience. Chairs sat behind them. There are old-school phones on the desks and stacks of files. One has a computer on as well. On the back wall there is a whiteboard and a cardboard-covered window. A yellowish glowing light peeks round the floppy edges of the cardboard. There is a banner somewhere with the name 'BRIGHTLINE' and some kind of tacky logo.

The walls are covered with posters/diagrams/cartoons for stuff like 'The Listening Wheel', 'Empathise, Don't Sympathise', 'Peer Pressure', 'Reasons to Be Cheerful', 'Today is the First Day of the Rest of Your Life', an acrostic poem of 'FRIENDSHIP', a massive plaque that says 'A Problem Shared is a Problem Halved'. Underneath and around the posters the walls are covered in damp/mould.

There is always a 'WORD OF THE WEEK' written on the whiteboard.

There's a hat stand by the door where everyone hangs their gas masks. The sound of rain is near-constant throughout the play. Every now and then a siren hurtles past.

Maybe a radio very quietly plays folk, rock and soul songs from the '60s and '70s – Bob Dylan, The Band, Tom Waits, Otis Redding, Leonard Cohen, Joni Mitchell, Etta James, Bruce Springsteen, Neil Young, The Rolling Stones.

The design shouldn't root us in a particular time. Some elements may seem retro, some modern, some futuristic. They should all be meshed together.

In fact, maybe everything that stays in the office – the computer, the phones, the posters, the songs on the radio, etc. – should feel kind of retro, from an analogue era. But everything that comes in from outside – the gas masks, smartphones, music emanating in from the takeaway next door, etc. – can feel modern or futuristic.

This text went to press before the end of rehearsals and so may differ slightly from the play as performed.

Week One

Lights up.

FRANCES, ANGIE and JOEY are each sitting at different desks. The kettle is on.

On the whiteboard is written: 'WORD OF THE WEEK – PERSEVERANCE!!'

FRANCES and ANGIE are both on the phone.

FRANCES. And what do you think it is that's making you feel this way?

JOEY just looks around, nervously.

Right.

He looks at the phone on his own desk.

Okay. Thank you for telling me that.

How does it feel to say that to someone?

He watches FRANCES and ANGIE on their calls.

How do you think she'd react if you said that to her?

The phone on his desk rings.
He looks over at FRANCES.
FRANCES nods. Maybe she gives him a big thumbs-up.

No, take your time. There's no rush.

ANGIE. Huh. So so just – sorry – Huh. Well I think maybe it might be helpful if you calmed down a little bit?

No I didn't mean –

(To herself.) Aw crap.

I'm sor–

I'm sor–

I'm sorry

Err. Yeah. No you're right when people tell you to calm down it can be very annoy–

5

JOEY *flicks through a notebook of useful phrases.*

JOEY *picks up his phone.*

JOEY. Hello, Brightline. You're

(*Clears his throat.*)

You're through to someone you can talk to.

He waits.

FRANCES *flashes* ANGIE *a look.*

That sounds really difficult. Have you always found it hard to talk to her about these kind of fears?

Do you mind if I call them fears?

Unhelpful! Yeah! That's the exact word I was thinking of as well! That's so funny we were… Errrrr but enough about me!

Okay how would you like to refer to it?

Concerns? Dilemmas?

Let's just – Huh. Okay I know I'll stop talking and you can just say whatever you want to say at whatever volume you think would work for you – whatever your favourite – *preferred* – level of… volume is.

JOEY *looks at* FRANCES *for reassurance.*

She signals for him to keep going.

Yeah. So um is…

Okay sure we can call them peeves. Peeves. I like that, you know. I might start calling my peeves, peeves. Fun to say, right!?

Um… Yes that is nice. Thank you?

Why don't you just say it a few times?

Peeves.

The kettle boils. FRANCES *goes to get it, dragging her phone with her.*

Huh.

Is there – like – anything you fancy chatting about or…?

Like…

Um…

The line goes dead. He puts the phone down.

(Mouthing to FRANCES.) They hung up.

JOEY nods.

JOEY grabs a piece of paper and starts doodling on it – sketching out a cartoon.

Exactly.

(Covering receiver.) Ange – tea?

How do you take yours, Joseph?

Peeves.

Peeves.

(Mouthing exaggeratedly to JOEY.) THAT'S OKAY! TEA?

(Back to phone.) Peeves. Yeah!

I think sometimes when you rename the problem you're dealing with it helps you put it in perspective.

Mmhmm.

Mmmm. Huh.

ANGIE winces and holds the phone further away from her ear.

Well it's a very stressful time isn't it.

Sorry yes.

But but but but what I mean is that I'm I'm I'm *sure* that they will understand you taking out that very understandable stress on on on them.

In answer to FRANCES, ANGIE pumps both fists in the air as if celebrating scoring a goal.

Huh.

It's Joey.

Mmm.

My name's… don't worry.

What?

Right. Huh. Tell me – tell me about that then.

Just a bit of milk?

Sugar?

Uh – no thanks.

Yeah.

(*Into phone.*) And in the dreams where does the blood come from?

Okay try to narrow it down for me.

(*Covering receiver, to* JOEY.) Yes to sugar?

Sure. Sugar. Yeah.

(*Mouthing.*) GREAT.

Ohhhhhh yeah. Yeah that's so funny I do that sometimes as well. So weird.

But they're not premonitions, they're just dreams. They're not based in anything real.

Sorry. Keep going.

Yes, I have.

Yes, I'm aware.

JON *enters from the door. He is wearing a gas mask and is soaked. He is slugging a trombone case on his back.* ANGIE *and* FRANCES *exchange a look of relief.*

He takes off his mask and coat.

JON *lets out a long groan of frustration.*

FRANCES *and* ANGIE *wave at him.*

JON. The bridges went down!

The others nod, grimly.

Jesus.

I had to drive like twenty miles north to get round it. Got stuck behind this little old lady in one of those old gas cars. Honestly the most confused human I've ever seen. She kept pulling up at these police stops like: 'So the bridge…

…down?'

'Yeah, babe. Bridge fell down. Bridge gone. Bridge no longer viable means of crossing.'

'OHHHHH' she says. Every single time.

'OHHHHH.' As if it's new – as if the full reality of the situation had just

No I know that kind of thing is happening – I just think it's, you know, important to look at the good things that are happening as well. And they might be small things but that doesn't invalidate them does it?

Mmm. But no there *are* some.

Well I think that's wonderful. Yes.

Huh. Yeah. I erm – no, go on.

No I was just gonna say that I feel that way all the time about my dog.

But it's probably different for a person isn't it – no you're right.

No no no no I wasn't trying to be disrespectful. Why would I *try* to…

Yeah. Yeah. Let's just pretend I didn't say that okay?

9

crystallised in front of her eyes and then twenty metres further down the road: 'So the bridge… fell… down.'

YES BETTY-LOU.

Fuck.

Sorry I'm late.

JON *registers* JOEY.

Who are you?

JOEY. I'm Joey.

JON. How old are you?

JOEY. I'm seventeen.

JON. Jesus.

JOEY (*cluelessly*)….yeah.

JON dumps his bag and goes to sit down at a desk. Maybe on the way he does some kind of secret handshake with ANGIE. He starts organising some papers.

Absolutely!

Okay so if that were to happen. If that were to take place – which I'm not saying it will – how do you think you'd react?

Okay well how do you think your wife would react?

No but I just want you to reason it through very slowly with me so that we both understand where you're coming from – does that sound –

The line goes dead.

Hello?

She turns to JON.

That sounds quite lonely.

No yeah scary as well. I meant scary really.

Huh.

Yep yep yep.

No – yeah and…

Huh. Well here we think it's important not to *lose* that hope.

To hold on to –

FRANCES. Hello Jon.

JON. Hey Frances. How was your week?

FRANCES. Yeah lovely actually. I think I made a really good point in one of my groups today –

JON. Oh yeah?

FRANCES. and I'm normally a bit shy there so I'm still feeling all buzzy from that.

(To JOEY.) I'm doing this masters in counselling at the moment.

JOEY. Oh cool.

FRANCES. Weather's been better than they said!

JON. It has.

FRANCES. I brought Jaffa Cakes!

JON *(to JOEY)*. Mummy brought Jaffa Cakes and the weather's getting better.

FRANCES. Sorry Joseph – / Jon's a

JON. It's Joey.

FRANCES. What?

JON. Says his name's Joey.

FRANCES. Oh?

JOEY. Yeah um… you know. Joseph/Joey – it's not really important

FRANCES. Well what would you prefer we call you?

Mmmm. I can understand and empathise with your situation.

ANGIE ticks off something on her notebook as she says 'understand' and 'empathise'.

And what does your wife say when you say that?

Okay.

JON. Joey – says his name's Joey.

FRANCES (to JOEY). What would you prefer?

Pause.

JOEY. Um… Joey yeah.

FRANCES. Right. Fab.

JOEY. But it's not really important.

FRANCES. No of / course it is

JOEY. My dad's name is Joseph so…

    it's…

    weird.

It sounds like you don't want to disappoint her maybe? But I might be reading too much…

FRANCES. Gosh that must be so weird!

JON. Is your dad a total dick or something?

FRANCES. Jon.

JOEY. Um…

No you're right I probably am. Yeah.

JON. I'm being such a twat tonight – christ. Do we have any coffee?

FRANCES. The cafetière needs a wash. / (To JOEY.) Chris's group are such mucky pups.

JON. I don't need the cafetière. Just that dirty dirty instant stuff.

    Fuck it's cold in here. Heater still broken?

FRANCES. I'm working on it. We're trying to get someone in who's um… in our price range.

Well I think we all feel that sometimes, yes. I mean I guess I can't

speak for other people but I feel that
yeah.

Well just exactly what you described.

Beat.

JON. You've lost another donor.

FRANCES. We're just being cautious.

JON. It's like the fucking *Titanic* at the moment.

FRANCES. It's nothing / to worry about.

JON. The people jumping off not the timeless love story – Dya want me on chat or calls?

FRANCES. Why don't you jump on chat for now until / we

Yeah and then I always get kind of
shaky. Like I get the shakes. Do you
get the shakes?

JON. Until I've achieved a more convincing zen?

FRANCES. No, I trust you entirely.

JON. Okay.

FRANCES. How was your week?

JON. Yeah fine.

FRANCES. Okay, then.

Huh.

JON. Me and Andy are moving house at the moment as well. So that's a fun additional nightmare.

FRANCES. That's exciting.

JON. Andy thinks so, yeah. A new era he calls it. A New Era, Joey.

13

14

JOEY. . . . cool.

JON. Spent Sunday trying to squeeze our mattress through the back window. It's like this metre-thick Posturepedic, lumbar-support thing. Literally saves my life on a night-by-night basis but it won't fit through a door. So me and Andy are just trying to squash this expanding fucking bouncy castle through our back window for about three hours. I'm just screaming the entire time and he's all do-de-do-de-do as always. It was a fresh hell.

JON pours himself a coffee, takes a sip straight away.

He winces at the burn.

God it's filthy but I love it.

JOEY's phone rings. He stares at it.

FRANCES nods encouragingly.

JOEY picks it up.

FRANCES puts on a headset so she can listen in.

JOEY. Someone you can talk –

Helloyou'rethroughtosomeoneyoucantalkto.

FRANCES. Slow down.

JOEY. Hi. This is Brightline.

Can I – Dya wanna talk to me about anything?

Yeah. Me too! There are like so many times that I've felt that way. I don't think I could count them. That's how many times there are.

Huh.

Well, for example, I'm a – by day I'm a teaching assistant so on Fridays I have to walk thirty kids to the swimming baths. And it's like a half-hour walk down a main road with no barriers so that feels pretty scary, pretty high-risk yeah. And the kids –

FRANCES. Ange.

JOEY. Well I think you just talk about whatever you want and…

Yeah.

/ Yeah one hundred per cent.

No I know it's not about me – I just thought we were talking about – having a conversation –

Wrap it up, Angie. Time to move on.

(*To* JOEY.) That's good, keep going.

Huh. Okay. Okay.

Okay.

So so I'm going to have to let you go but but

BUT I WANT YOU TO KNOW THAT YOU CAN CALL BACK AT ANY TIME IF YOU NEED TO TALK TO SOMEONE ABOUT THIS.

Okay. Yeah I understand and empathise with how you feel – your situation

Thank you.

Thank you.

JON *turns to watch* ANGIE. *He slurps his coffee.*

Okay bye bye now.

Okay – yeah

Well what does she –

Have a nice –

15

Have a –

Have a –

Have a nice –

Haveaniceday!

She slams the phone down.

Mmm.

Pause.

JON *and* FRANCES *watch* ANGIE.

JON *holds back a laugh.*

She doesn't meet their gaze.

Eventually:

FRANCES. I thought you handled that really well, Angie.

ANGIE. Yeah.

FRANCES. You were controlled and disciplined and you were listening very actively. Great job!

ANGIE. Thanks Frances.

FRANCES. I think if there's any tiny tiny little room for improvement or development

ANGIE. Yeah.

FRANCES. It would be A) let's steer away from those personal anecdotes.

ANGIE. Yeah definitely.

FRANCES. And B) let's try not letting *their* emotional energy influence *your* emotional energy.

ANGIE. Yeah I was thinking that – that's so funny that you said that because I was just thinking that.

JON. Well done, Ange.

ANGIE. Thanks Jon. I'm sorry that the bridges fell down.

JON. Thanks, Ange.

FRANCES. Joey.

FRANCES goes back and listens in to JOEY's call.

Well she sounds like a – like a fucking bitch right?

JOEY. No no I didn't mean that in a –

I just meant that because you were angry with / her so –

FRANCES. Calm.

JOEY. Sorry I didn't mean to –

I'm not –

Look I'm not trying to insult your fucking mum, man. I'm just saying you don't have to like live in *fear* just cos she

Phone goes dead.

Silence. They all look at JOEY.

Her mum was like – manipulating… like telling her how to…

Never mind.

Pause.

FRANCES. A really great first go, I reckon.

Right everyone?

ANGIE. Definitely. Yep.   JON. Oh yeah.

FRANCES. Let's go for less swearing though.

JOEY. Yeah. Sorry, miss.

FRANCES. Frances.

JOEY. Frances.

Pause.

FRANCES. I'm gonna get the Jaffa Cakes!

FRANCES *exits.*

(*From off.*) Great job you guys!

Silence.

ANGIE *turns away and starts arranging some papers.*

JON. Listen, I know in training they go on and on about not swearing on the phones but sometimes it does help set them at ease, you know.

JOEY. Oh cool. Yeah. Um / – *training?*

JON. Yeah it's something you pick up – just feel it out.

JOEY. Thanks.

JON. You're seventeen.

JOEY. Yeah.

JON. Brill.

JON turns back to his computer. ANGIE picks a tissue out of a box and blows her nose a little too loudly.

ANGIE plucks another tissue out of the box.

She starts giggling. She leans over to JOEY.

ANGIE. Hey Joey.

JOEY. ... What?

ANGIE. I was just thinking. Uh. Like. How cool is it that when you pick a tissue out of a tissue box another one just comes right up, ready to be picked next.

JOEY. Uh. Yeah?

ANGIE. Imagine, like, when they were designing the tissues and like – this whole team of people – this team of Crack Engineers from like *NASA* trying all these different folds, doing loads of like *mathematical* calculations and measurements to find a way to make the next tissue come up when you pull one out. Months and months and *years* of research and like *equations* go into it. Millions of tissues just folded wrong and THROWN INTO THE FIRE. And then they all gather around this one tissue box, in the lab or whatever, and one of them just reaches out a hand, pulls a tissue from the box and...

ANGIE plucks a tissue from the box.

They're like: 'YAAAAAASSSS! COME ON!' They're all hugging and kissing each other.

YEAAAAAAH! AHHHHHHHhhhhhhhhhhhhhh!

19

She tails off.

Pause.

JOEY. Uh yeah?

ANGIE. …just would've been a pretty cool room to be in.

Never-mind though.

ANGIE shrinks away. JON is typing on the keyboard.

JOEY turns to look at the whiteboard.

He reads the word of the week.

Turns back to his desk.

They're all sitting at different angles – their backs to each other.

FRANCES walks past the door humming to herself.

All in their own worlds.

Suddenly the kettle explodes.

Everyone screams and dives under the tables. Chaos:

JON. WHAT THE FUCK WAS THAT?

ANGIE. I DON'T KNOW / I DON'T KNOW

FRANCES (*shouting from off*). WHAT HAPPENED? / EVERYONE OKAY? JOEY?

JOEY. I think it was the kettle. IT'S THE KETTLE.

FRANCES (*shouting from off*). The one in here's gone too.

*

FRANCES *sits in the centre of the room blowing up a huge, brightly coloured beach ball. Everyone else watches her.* JON *is sat by the computer.* ANGIE *and* JOEY *are stood up – ready.*

She struggles to blow it up.

It takes a while.

FRANCES *takes a breath and the ball goes down a lot.*

JON *groans. She starts blowing again. Eventually:*

FRANCES. OOOOOKAY!

Jon?

JON *stands, reluctantly.*

They stand in a circle.

Ready?

General murmurs.

Okay.

FRANCES *throws the ball into the air and, as she bats it, shouts:*

What would you say to someone in your position!

They play a game of Keep It Up shouting a useful phone phrase whenever the ball comes to them – all straight out of the guidebook. Below is a list of phrases they say. This bit should be different every night. JOEY *sometimes panics and repeats ones that have already been said.*

ALL. What's going on in your head at the moment!

Have you felt able to talk to anyone else!

Where are you calling me from!

What name would you like me to call you!

When we've finished talking, what do you think you'll do next!

How long have you been feeling this way!

How often do you think about the things that *haven't* fallen apart yet!

Tap the phone so I know you can hear me!

If you were to talk to someone how would it feel!

I understand and empathise with how you're feeling!

What options have you thought about!

What do you think they'd say if they knew how you felt!

What's brought you to us today!

If you had to look for positives what would they be!

Everything is going to be okay!

As this goes on and phrases begin to be repeated, JOEY starts to say –

JOEY. Hello, Brightline. You're through to someone you can talk to.

– every time the ball comes to him in an increasingly garbled fashion.

A phone rings.

FRANCES. KEEP GOING!

She answers the phone at the same time JOEY hits the ball.

JOEY *and* FRANCES. Hello Brightline, you're through to someone you can talk to.

FRANCES. Hi Geoff. What's brought you to us today?

Okay.

The next time the ball comes to JON, he palms it straight down into the ground.

*

JON and ANGIE are on the phone.

JOEY is helping FRANCES carry a big box of files out of the room.

JON. Alright, mate. Let it out yeah.

ANGIE. Well you say that but maybe with um… you know… with a bit of perspective it won't feel so overwhelming.

Well why don't you describe to me what, in an ideal world – What was his name did you say?

Oh that's a nice name – did you choose it?

Yeah. So why don't you describe what, in your mind, Shane's life would look like.

Quickly. Why don't you describe it to me really quickly.

South for university. Yep. And who would he meet there?

FRANCES. Okay guys let's wrap it up – debrief time.

Gonna have to wrap them up. Let's go.

Ange.

(*Hand over receiver.*) I've got a weeper.

Listen mate I'm gonna have to leave you. But I'm really proud of you for

23

Ange.

Ange stop now please.

ANGIE.

Pause.

FRANCES *is gripping her stomach with both hands – the baby is kicking hard.*

JOEY *notices.*

Sorry, Angie but we really need to save enough time for the debrief. It's super important.

JOEY. Miss, are you okay?

FRANCES. Oh yeah, just got a bit of a kicker on board!

JOEY. whoa

letting all of this out alright? Alright now. Yeah mop yourself up and get back into bed. Stay safe alright?

Someone with a bit of fire?

ANGIE *giggles.*

That's sweet. Where would they settle?

Oh it's so nice up there. He could go camping at the weekends.

Oh wow. And they have one of those model villages too and they're always nice.

Hi Cathy. Errr I'm really sorry. I need to go now but this has been so so great to... like so so cool –

She hung up.

JON. Bit cruel that I reckon, Ange.

ANGIE. What?

JON. Describe your son's perfect future.

FRANCES. Whenever I get kinda riled... Errrr okay then team! What a good session! Let's all give ourselves some back-pats. Really good atmosphere I reckon. Really intelligent, empathetic listening. And what a debut from our young star!

FRANCES cheers. The others reluctantly cheer along.

JOEY cheers awkwardly.

JON. Give us a bow mate.

JOEY *laughs.*

No go on.

Go on.

JOEY awkwardly bows.

JON cheers very loudly.

FRANCES. Okay so – Ooft this is a big one.

The baby is kicking harder.

JOEY. Is it a boy or a girl?

FRANCES. We want it to be a surprise. Blimey. Guys come feel this!

Beat. The others look at each other uncertainly.

Seriously get over here!

ANGIE and JOEY shrug, go over and put their hands on FRANCES's stomach.

JON turns away, averting his eyes.

FRANCES looks at JON, sadly.

ANGIE. Why?

JOEY. whoa.

FRANCES. Right?

JOEY. Miss. There's… there's a person in your tummy.

ANGIE. It's like you've got a fish tank with one of those big tropical fish in it except it's like IN your stomach not on a shelf or… or a counter.

FRANCES *beams at them.*

JOEY. I haven't seen a pregnant lady since I was like twelve.

FRANCES *looks down.*

JOEY *withdraws.*

Oh… sorry.

FRANCES *smiles at him and shakes her head: don't worry.*

An awkward moment then ANGIE *withdraws.*

FRANCES. So. Is there anything anyone would like to leave here? At the end of every week Joey we ask if there's anything anyone wants to get off their chest. Anything that's happened here this evening that you'd like not to carry with you into the outside world. So…

Pause.

Nothing? Everyone's completely fine and dandy?

Pause.

JOEY. feels like we're about to do a huddle or something – some kind of chant.

FRANCES. We could do a huddle? Bring it in guys?

She starts to initiate a huddle but immediately senses reluctance.

Or let's just, you know, let's just *hang* where we are. Stay cool! So nobody's got anything to…

Awkward pause.

Well that is great. Aren't we all tough cookies.

Okay let's go have ourselves some good weeks and I'll see you back here next Tuesday night.

Pause. They give each other a couple of supportive nods as if to say: stay safe. JON breaks away first.

JON. Cheers Frances.

ANGIE. Thanks / Frances.

JOEY. Cheers.

ANGIE (*to FRANCES*). Can I just run to the loo before you lock up?

FRANCES nods. ANGIE runs out. Everyone else goes to pack up their bags. This takes as long as it takes.

FRANCES. Oh Joey I'm supposed to sign your work-experience form?

JOEY. Oh yeah.

He hands her a form, watches as she signs it then folds it up and puts it back in his bag.

FRANCES carries a load of files out and down the corridor.

JON hauls his trombone case onto his shoulder.

What's that?

JON. It's a trombone.

JOEY. Oh cool.

JON. I'm not being a prick or anything, bringing it in – it's just this is a crap neighbourhood and I feel a bit dodgy leaving it in the car.

27

JOEY. Right yeah.

They resume packing. Pause.

I used to play a bit of bassoon.

JON. *Very* cool.

JOEY. Yeah.

JON. My husband makes me take lessons Tuesday evenings with this old guy in Denly which means lugging this bloody thing to work, to Denly and then to here every week.

JOEY. Effort.

JON. Yeah. (*Finished packing up.*) Alright mate.

JOEY. Why does he make you take lessons? Is he like a big-band player or something?

JON *laughs*.

JON. Uh. No. That'd be funny if you knew him. He um…

He wanted me to 'actively engage in something Positive'.

JOEY. And you picked trombone?

JON. Yeah. He hates the trombone. Now he has to hear me stumble through 'Ode to Joy' over and over again every evening before bed.

He's one of *her* types, you know. Made me quit smoking. And I loved smoking.

JOEY *laughs*.

JON. Alright mate.

JOEY. Yeah see ya later.

JON. Keep your feet on the ground yeah?

JOEY. Uh yeah? Yeah.

FRANCES *comes back in. JON doesn't notice.*

JON. I know we're supposed to be all – you know – but don't let her float you off into the clouds, youknowwhatImean.

JOEY . . . . yeah.

JON *turns round to see* FRANCES *standing in the doorway.*

An awkward pause.

JON. Stay safe, guys.

FRANCES. Absolutely!

JON *leaves – gas mask on, grabs a newspaper from a pile to hold over his head.*

FRANCES *goes to say something then stops herself.*

She resumes packing up.

JOEY *hesitates, gas mask on the top of his head.*

JOEY. Uh miss? – Frances sorry.

FRANCES. Yeah?

JOEY. I'm not supposed to have like –

Jon kept talking about training and…

I swear I wasn't trying to skip anything – / I didn't know – nobody told me – I might've missed an email or…

FRANCES. No no. Oh bless you. No Joey um – we were… so impressed with your application that we that we decided to um – to put you straight through. That you could learn on the job. And I'm so glad we did because you're learning so fast!

29

JOEY. Oh.

FRANCES. Yeah.

JOEY. Okay. Cool.

FRANCES. SO cool.

Pause. FRANCES *beams at him.*

JOEY. Frances – do you genuinely like… think everything's gonna…

FRANCES. What?

JOEY. Never mind.

Pause.

FRANCES. How do you get home?

JOEY. A couple of night buses.

FRANCES. You live in Wide Oak right?

JOEY. Yeah – well ish – just south of there.

FRANCES. I'll give you a lift.

JOEY. Oh uh. I don't wanna put you out or anything.

FRANCES. No it's on / my way.

JOEY. Bus is really easy.

FRANCES *throws* JOEY *her car keys.*

FRANCES. Can you go turn the heating on while I pack up here? I like it when it's nice and toasty. It's the yellow one.

Beat.

JOEY. Okay.

Thanks Frances.

JOEY exits.

FRANCES hurriedly clears a few files.

Once that's done she waits for a moment.

She puts her hands on her stomach and looks down at it.

A moment.

She exits.

FRANCES (*calling after him*). You know Joseph is on our baby-name list!

Pause.

ANGIE runs back in to find nobody there.

Blackout.

31

Week Two

Lights up.

On the whiteboard is written: 'WORD OF THE WEEK – GENEROSITY!!!'

JOEY and ANGIE sit facing each other. FRANCES is behind JOEY, massaging his shoulders as if prepping him for a fight.

JON is off to the side organising a gigantic, messy pile of DBS folders. There's a ball sitting on JON's desk. He bounces it every now and then when thinking.

FRANCES. Alright alright alright! Here we go, champ.

ANGIE holds her hand to her ear in the shape of a phone. She makes a phone-ringing sound.

ANGIE. *Bring bring!*

An actual phone rings. FRANCES goes to it.

ANGIE and JOEY exchange a glance as if to say: weird timing.

FRANCES. Hello, Brightline. You're through to –

Hi, sorry no this is a helpline can you take us off your register please?

Oh well for anyone really. But particularly if you feel at all overwhelmed by recent…

Oh great! Well why don't you give us a call back when you are on your own time and we can have a little chat.

Fab.

Yep thanks a bunch. What was your name, love?

Okay you have a nice day now. Yeah.

Puts phone down.

FRANCES. Okay let's go!

ANGIE. *Bring bring!*

Another actual phone rings. FRANCES goes to it.

ANGIE looks down at her hands as if she has magical powers.

Whoa.

FRANCES. Hello, Bright–

Puts the phone down.

Dead.

JON goes to the back of the room where the kettle used to be, heaps a couple of spoonfuls of instant coffee into his mug, then realises there is no kettle.

He pauses for a moment.

He tips the instant coffee into his mouth and chews.

Returns to his seat and resumes sorting.

One more time.

Wait Jon, you okay?

JON *nods.*

FRANCES *nods at* ANGIE.

ANGIE *takes a deep breath in as if preparing for a penalty kick.*

ANGIE. *Bring bring!*

Pause. They wait for a phone to ring. Nothing.

FRANCES *nods at* JOEY.

JOEY *makes his hand into a phone shape and raises it to his ear.*

JOEY. Hello, Brightline? You're through to someone who can speak to you – talk to.

ANGIE (*to* FRANCES). Anything I want?

FRANCES. Sure.

ANGIE (*putting on a deep, gravelly voice, to* JOEY). 'Hey baby.'

FRANCES. Oh Ange, / let's try a

ANGIE. You said anything.

FRANCES. I know / but let's –

JON. Go on. He's gotta get used to it.

Beat.

JOEY. Err hello. How are you today?

ANGIE *starts stroking her thigh.*

ANGIE. 'I'm good baby, how are you doing?'

JOEY. Yeah really good, thanks. Is there something you'd like to talk to me about?

ANGIE. 'There are so many things I'd like to talk to you about baby I can't even count 'em.'

NO! No – wait lemme go again.

'Yeah we could talk but your words would look so much better on my floor.'

NO!

'I didn't come here to talk.'

JOEY. Um come where – where are you right now?

ANGIE. Errrrrrrrrrrr 'I'm in your bedroom baby.'

JOEY. Whoa.

JOEY *turns his chair away from* ANGIE.

ANGIE. 'I'm I'm I'm all over your bedroom baby.'

JOEY. Okay now.

ANGIE. 'Mmmmm I'm rubbing my whole body over all your clothes and your pyjamas, all your files and folders. Mmmm I'm putting them in my mouth.'

JOEY. You're putting my files and folders in your mouth?

FRANCES. Go on Joey.

JOEY. Why – why – why are you doing that?

ANGIE. 'Cos it feels so good baby.'

JOEY. Oh god.

FRANCES *leans down and whispers in* JOEY's *ear.*

It's interesting to me that you feel the need to talk in this manner?

FRANCES. Great.

ANGIE. 'Oh yeah? You find it interesting? You find it real interesting? Let me tell you what else is interesting. My gigantic –'

JON *laughs to himself.*

FRANCES *shoots him a disapproving look.*

JOEY (*standing up*). nope.

    ANGIE *giggles*.

FRANCES. Okay.

JOEY (*to* ANGIE). Why did you do that?

    ANGIE *giggles*.

FRANCES. Okay what Angie was simulating there –

JOEY. She was like –

FRANCES. Yep.

JOEY. She was having a wank.

FRANCES. The character that Angie was portraying there was performing masturbation, yes.

JOEY. Why!?

FRANCES. Well, Joey, lots of people think it's appropriate to call us as a means of achieving further arousal.

JOEY. That's fucked up.

FRANCES. It is yeah. It's horrible / actually –

JON. Frances *hates* them.

FRANCES. I do hate it but um / there's definitely a

JON. She thinks the baby can hear them.

FRANCES. I don't think the baby can hear them.

JOEY. Well why d'you do it to me then?

ANGIE. I just thought it'd be funny.

Beat.

FRANCES. So Joey these are pretty common. We try to resist hanging up immediately – that's Brightline policy, unfortunately. It's possible that these callers may be testing the service out and that they may actually need us at a... at a future date so –

ANGIE. So like a group of teenagers will ring up and just be like: SUCK MY DICK and I'll just be like: 'Why do you feel like saying that to me?'

JOEY. Whoa.

ANGIE. 'SUCK MY BIG HAIRY DICK.' – So what's making you feel this way?

FRANCES. Thanks Angie.

ANGIE. 'PUT IT IN YOUR WET DRIPPING CUNT.' – How's your mum?

FRANCES. OKAY!

Pause.

They're good examples. Great examples.

ANGIE. People just need an outlet don't they?

FRANCES (*almost involuntarily*). No.

ANGIE *and* JOEY *look at* FRANCES *weirdly.*

Jon are they the DBS folders?

FRANCES *goes over to help him.*

JOEY *gets out a lunchbox and starts eating a sandwich. There is a cartoon sticker on the lunchbox.*

JON. Yeah they're a mess.

FRANCES. I know. Chris just dumps them in here completely unsorted.

37

ANGIE *picks up the lunchbox to read the cartoon.*

ANGIE. That's cool. I like that.

JOEY. …my mum got it me.

ANGIE. Sorry if I like… embarrassed you.

JOEY (*turning away from her*). Yeah. It's fine. I'm just trying really hard so…

ANGIE. Oh I'm really sorry Joey.

JOEY'*s phone rings.*

JOEY. Hello Brightline, you're through to someone you can talk to.

FRANCES *goes over.*

FRANCES. Ange can I…?

FRANCES *takes* ANGIE'*s seat and puts on a headset to listen in to* JOEY'*s call.*

ANGIE *stands where she is for a moment, not knowing where to go.*

FRANCES *smiles and nods at her.* ANGIE *moves away.*

JOEY. Okay well tell me about that then.

Yeah. I um – yeah.

Well – well – if it's making you feel that way why do you keep – why do you FEEL THE NEED (*Looks at* FRANCES *for approval.*) to keep doing it?

Um…

FRANCES. Don't say your real name.

FRANCES *and* JON *sort the files together.*

JON'*s desk phone rings.*

JON. Hello Brightline. You're through to someone you can talk to.

Okay.

JOEY. It's… Gavin.

Um

FRANCES *shakes her head.*

I am fifty-seven years of age.

Uh well it's easy. You just go: Okay well I'm just gonna think about the next half an hour not the next five years and then uh when that half-hour is up you just start again and repeat ad… infinitum?

FRANCES *nods, impressed.*

I think it means 'to infinity'. My mum's using a lot of Latin phrases at the moment. I think she thinks it makes her sound authorita–

FRANCES *is giving him a warning glance.*

But uh how do you – what dya think of the half-hour thing?

It's not stupid.

JOEY *starts watching* JON.

Alright slow down for me mate
There you go.

Right okay.

No not at all. That's good. What's your name, pal?

Wait. Stevie?

Mate! It's Jon!

The very same. HI MATE! How on earth are you?

Yeah well we get all the local calls first. There's like a switchboard thing so –

Every Tuesday night yeah. For a little while now.

39

It's alright you know. You get some dickheads. But –

Beat.

Listen mate we're not really allowed to talk to people we recognise on here. Gotta be anonymous and all that. But we should all grab a beer soon yeah?

FRANCES (*to* JON). Jon.

Jon come on.

Great. And you're – you know – you're alright yeah?

Cool. Yeah that's between me and you. Won't go anywhere.

Mmhmm.

Jon, hang up the call please.

I'm sorry about that, I should've recognised your voice earlier.

Cheers Stevie. Sorry.

Yeah. That makes sense too I guess. But maybe my way's worth a go?

JON *puts the phone down.*

Yep. I know.

Yeah. No I'm with you.

JON *winces, runs his hands through his hair.*

Jon.

JON *gets up and goes to the toilet.*

I'm not saying it's not really hard. I think it's really really hard but –

No that's not what I meant.

Well

Uh.

Yeah we are a listening service – you just asked me for advice so I gave advice.

Wait –

Phone goes dead.

FRANCES. Great job, Joey!

JOEY. Yeah.

FRANCES. You've got to remember that ninety per cent of these calls don't end in 'thank you so much, you've made me feel so much better'. Most people just hang up.

JOEY. Yeah.

FRANCES. But they *really* appreciate it.

JOEY. Yeah.

JON re-enters and heads to his desk.

FRANCES. I think maybe let's rein it in when we say our age? You've got such a big booming, manly deep voice but I don't know if it quite sounds fifty-seven yet. Maybe soon though!

JOEY. Yeah that makes sense.

FRANCES (*turning to* JON). Um Jon I can't have you breaching –

JON (*snapping*). I KNOW.

Beat. JON *takes a breath.*

I get it, Frances.

41

Pause. JON *fiddles with the ball.*

FRANCES. Joey, it was so great to meet your mum last week by the way.

JOEY. Yeah. She said you seemed really nice.

FRANCES. Didn't wake her up did we?

JON *watches* FRANCES *and* JOEY.

JOEY. No. She um – she always makes sure she's up when I get home. She works early mornings anyway so…

FRANCES. Nice. And how are you getting on with all those Nasty Decisions?

JOEY. Yeah uh… Okay? I guess. I was thinking about… I really like cartoons. Comics and stuff. So I was thinking about maybe looking into some course about that?

FRANCES. Oh wow. That sounds great.

JOEY. Yeah?

FRANCES. So creative!

JOEY. Uh yeah. I'm not a very imaginative person or anything. But yeah.

FRANCES. Great stuff, Joe! Why don't you start working on a personal statement and I'll read it next week!

JOEY. Um.

FRANCES. SUCH an exciting time.

JOEY. Yeah. I hadn't really um… But I guess it is, yeah.

FRANCES. I'm gonna get us some treats.

JOEY. Cool.

FRANCES *exits.*

JOEY *smiles to himself.*

Pause.

JON *throws* JOEY *the ball.*

*

JON *and* JOEY *are throwing the ball between them, across the room.*

ANGIE *is still on the computer.*

JON. It's the worst, it's the worst, man. People lose their minds at you. Today I was on an evaluation, this nine-year-old girl bounded up to me. Real cute – pigtails, little… kinda bow thing. I was like: Hi! And then she told me to go fuck myself.

JOEY. Whoa. Why?

JON. Her family's house went down and I couldn't sign off on it.

JOEY. Shit.

JON. Yeah.

JOEY. What do you say to that?

JON. I'm like babe, of course I wanna give you your money. I wanna build your house back up with my bare fingers. I wanna cut my arm off just to feel like I am *doing* something to *help* you but I am a tiny puny pawn in a large large insurance conglomerate – I've got no authority to approve your claim.

Not that anybody knows what to do with these claims now anyway.

Course you can't really explain this to a nine-year-old.

JOEY. Where was this?

43

JON. This is round by Gorely.

JOEY. It's bad there right?

JON. Yeah we get a lot of calls from round there.

Beat.

JOEY. Was that your friend calling before?

JON. Stevie yeah. Well I don't know him that well. He's my mate Jenna's little brother.

JOEY. That's kinda awkward.

JON. Yeah I should've… You gotta hang up if you recognise them really. Compromises them, compromises you. I should've realised.

JOEY. Are you gonna tell his sister he called?

JON. Can't.

JOEY. Yeah.

Pause.

I used to go swimming near Gorely.

JON. Yeah people are still doing that! It's horrible – the sea is this kinda grey colour and it's thick and stewy / and

JOEY. Viscous.

JON. Yeah viscous.

JOEY *gags.*

But people are still swimming.

JOEY. Sometimes we uh... we did some bodyboarding? pretty fun.

JON. Didn't see any bodyboarders but I'll let you know.

JOEY. Thanks.

Beat.

JON. That's such a school word – viscous. I haven't heard anyone say viscous in like ten years.

JOEY. Yeah.

Beat.

JOEY. My chemistry teacher has this really bad lisp. So he says um, he says – 'vishcush' .

JON. 'Vishcush'

JOEY. 'Vishcush'

JON. 'Vishcush'

JOEY. Yeah.

JON. That's funny, man.

JOEY ....yeah.

Pause.

JON. So you're finishing up at school at the moment.

JOEY. Yeah.

JON. What's next?

JOEY. Dunno.

45

JON. Weird atmosphere?

JOEY. What?

JON. In school.

JOEY. Errr. Yeah? Kind of.

JON. Hard.

JOEY. What?

JON. Working towards…

JOEY. Yeah.

I dunno.

School's okay.

Pause.

JON. What?

JOEY. …my mum says that when you're a teenager, everything feels like the end of the world.

JON. Yeah.

I'm thirty-two.

JOEY. Yeah.

Frances's kid's gonna be like…

JON. Yup.

JOEY. It's her first right?

JON. Yeah. I can't...

He shakes his head. Pause. They throw the ball back and forth for a while. The sound of ANGIE typing on the keyboard.

JOEY. Do you get to choose what pieces you learn?

JON. What?

JOEY. On the trombone.

JON. Err I don't really play 'pieces' yet. I just do kind of exercises and basic tunes.

JOEY. Oh right.

JON. Arpeggios.

JOEY. Yeah.

JON. Why?

JOEY *shrugs.*

JOEY. I used to have lessons but I don't really have them any more.

JON. Such a pain.

JOEY. Yeah.

JON. You're at St Catherine's right?

JOEY. Bartholomew's.

JON. OH MY GOD. You are such a St Bart's kid. YES. Literally everything about you makes sense to me now.

JOEY. What does that mean?

JON. Come on St Bart's kids all have that same kinda smell.

47

JOEY. What smell?

JON. You all have The Smell.

JOEY. I don't have / The Smell.

JON. Oh my god I used to fucking HATE kids from that school. Me and Andy are moving into this new place down the road from Bart's. I keep seeing you guys just… fucking… going into shops. It's like being haunted.

JOEY. Oh where's / your new

JON. You were all fucking self-important and self-righteous and had kinda weird hair. Like you all had a really anal thing about your hair. People touching it / and

JOEY. I'm completely fine with people touching my hair.

JON. Sure.

JOEY. You went to Cat's?

JON. Atley College. My sister went to Cat's – lucky bitch.

JOEY. You went to At Col.

JON. *At. Col…?* That is so 'youth of today' of you.

JOEY. What?

JON. I mean must we abbreviate everything these days? Must we? Ange, touch his hair.

ANGIE *pulls herself away from the computer and goes over to mess up JOEY's hair.*

JOEY *(evading* ANGIE*).* Errrrrrrrr. Seriously? / Seriously?

JON. Oh man – I used to hang out in the um – above your canteen hall there's like, or there used to be, this kind of little attic thing. Basically a loft that everyone had just forgotten was there. We used to go up there and smoke and like *tentatively* feel each other up.

JOEY. I thought you hated Bart's kids.

JON. Yeah but I was sixteen – I didn't exactly live or die by my principles. A couple of your teachers used to come up sometimes. My mate had this threesome with this guy who was in for supply.

JOEY. Wait wait wait wait wait – what teacher?

JON. Um I think his name was like Thorn/…ford?

JOEY. Thornburg!?

JON. Yeah!

JOEY. WHAT

JON. What?

JOEY. Thornburg's like an urban legend. Holy shit. Apparently he ran some horrible sex-orgy dungeon with his students.

JON. Nah that's such bullshit. He had like one fumbly threesome with my mate Vinny and some girl on foreign exchange.

JOEY. …I mean everyone says he had a *dungeon*.

JON. Ohhhh that is SO Bart's. You guys blow everything way out of proportion.

JON starts laughing to himself.

Rein it right back in, lads.

JON keeps laughing.

JOEY. Well um… we all say At Col kids are a bit: 'ahhhhhhhhh'

JOEY sticks his tongue out and shakes his head around a bit while saying: 'ahhhhhh'.

Beat.

49

JON. Well that's just mean.

JOEY. I can't believe you knew Horny Thornburg. He's a legend.

JON. *He* is a legend? That's like the most depressing thing I've ever heard.

JOEY grins.

They throw the ball back and forth for a while.

JOEY. Where did you go to school, Angie?

ANGIE doesn't respond – too focused on the screen ahead of her.

JON. Ange?

ANGIE. Oh. Sorry. What?

JOEY. Where did you go to school?

ANGIE. Oh. Errr. All over really.

FRANCES enters carrying a huge tray of doughnuts.

FRANCES. Okay potatoes! I've got mainly jam cos I know that's what you guys like but I got a couple of vanillas because I knew I wanted a vanilla but that none of you guys really like vanilla but then I got really panicked that you'd see me having a vanilla one and think I was being really selfish so I got two vanillas just in case.

Beat.

JON. I'll have a jam.

ANGIE. Me too please!

FRANCES throws them each a doughnut. They tuck in.

FRANCES. Joey?

Vanilla or jam?

Pause.

They are sat facing each other for a debrief session.

Silence.

FRANCES. Nothing? Nobody wants to leave anything here?

Jon?

JON *shakes his head.*

Pause.

How are we all feeling about everything?

General nods.

GREAT!

FRANCES *beams at everyone for a moment.*

Okay I think I'd like to… I'd like to leave something here. If that's okay with you guys. I errr… Huh.

She steadies herself.

I spoke to a little girl on the phone today who had um – she was in care, social care, and she was basically just shouting about the care home – like 'THEY'RE NOT THE BOSS OF ME', apparently they kept telling her when to go to the toilet and everything. And she was really angry. She was really angry that they had that control over her. 'THEY CAN'T TELL ME WHEN TO GO TO THE TOILET.' She'd been taken into care because her mum had uh… had had a vision of God. Or *a* god. Her mum thought she'd had a vision of *a* god telling her to go to Guadalajara in Mexico? Which I actually went to once and is a really lovely place, really good zoo. But yes – and to go on her own – not to take the little girl with her. And that that's where he,

51

God, would find her and and tell her what he needed her to do. But she had to go alone. She couldn't take anyone with her. So she left the little girl – this girl I was speaking to – outside a hospital and took off. But well… the thing is, the girl on the phone wasn't angry at her mum at all. She just loved her. She's just totally head over heels in love with her. And she couldn't stop going on about this care-home person called Sally who stopped her going to the toilet during dinnertime. Kept ranting and ranting about Sally. She'd hiss and spit her name out like: sssally. sssally. sssally. sssally. sssally.

Silence.

Great! Thanks for listening to me there. Feels great to get that off my chest. SO good we have these!

She beams at them all once more.

Well let's all go out there and have great weeks.

And get some good sleep.

They all go to pack up their stuff. JOEY hands FRANCES his form to sign. She does so.

Oh yes. Oh oh oh! Next week is Angie's six months! So we'll have a little do. Sound good?

JOEY. Is six months a big deal or something?

FRANCES. They say that if you're here for six months, you'll be here the rest of your life. Well done, Angie.

JON. Well done, Ange.

JOEY. Well done.

ANGIE *smiles.*

FRANCES. Can't wait to celebrate with you all.

JON exits. JOEY checks that he's gone then:

JOEY. Uh Frances am I okay to get a lift again?

FRANCES. Yeah of course.

She throws him the keys.

JOEY. And you can uh… You can come in for a cup of tea when we get there if you want?

Beat.

FRANCES. I would love that.

JOEY exits. FRANCES grins, grabs her stuff and makes to leave.

ANGIE has been hesitating.

ANGIE. Frances?

FRANCES. Yep?

ANGIE. Um. It's totally okay if you say no to this but I was wondering if next week I could be on the phone more? Instead of the chat. Just seeing as it's my six months.

FRANCES. Oh gosh you were on that all night weren't you?

ANGIE. Yeah. Pretty much.

FRANCES. Sorry, Angie. I must've got distracted.

ANGIE. That's okay.

FRANCES. Great

ANGIE. I just think I'm better at connecting with them on the phone.

FRANCES. Okay.

ANGIE. It's like – when we're on the phone – there's this string holding us together. Like when you were a kid and you / made those

53

54

FRANCES. Okay, Ange.

Beat.

ANGIE. Thanks Frances.

Blackout.

Week Three

On the whiteboard is written: 'WORD OF THE WEEK – UNDERSTANDING!!!'

All of the posters have fallen off the walls to reveal huge patches of damp and mould. Maybe some cracks in the wall as well? Pipes?

ANGIE is alone in the office, trying to put the posters back up.

She does this in silence for a while.

Then she looks around.

She runs to the door and peeks her head around it, scanning for anyone there. Nobody.

She returns to the poster.

Then, very softly she begins singing 'La Vie en rose' by Édith Piaf.

Initially it's too quiet to tell what song it is but, as she goes on it gets very slightly louder – never full-volume though, always just about under her breath. She's not very good at singing. Lots of the notes are a bit strained. Maybe she does really small, subtle dance moves – a flick of the wrist, a sway of the hips.

She has gotten through most of the song when she hears FRANCES's voice and immediately falls silent again.

FRANCES (*offstage*). Okay well, Harry, if you want to use money that *you've* earned to

FRANCES walks past the door, down the corridor, wearing her gas mask. We hear her turn a tap on.

I'm not being unsupportive. I'm really super proud that you got it written but I don't –

55

Like if you were a a a Heroin Addict and you asked me to buy you some Heroin then I, as someone that cared about you, wouldn't do that.

Okay.

I'm sorry I didn't mean to be inflammatory. Maybe it wasn't a good analogy. But –

FRANCES walks round the door, into the room. She has her gas mask propped on the top of her forehead.

She notices ANGIE.

Angie.

ANGIE. Hi.

FRANCES. You're here early.

ANGIE. Yeah – sorry is that…?

FRANCES. No – no problem.

(*Into phone.*) Hi Harry, listen I'm going to have to go.

We can talk about this at breakfast.

I love –

Oh.

She puts the phone down, takes off her coat and gas mask, smiles at ANGIE.

What happened to all the posters?

ANGIE. When I got in the cardboard was off the window and the wind had…

It was like an air tunnel in here.

FRANCES. Whoa.

ANGIE. Yeah.

Pause.

FRANCES *goes to help* ANGIE *stick the posters up.*

FRANCES. Good week?

ANGIE. It was nice. You?

FRANCES. Yeah. Great. Thank you.

Have you tried that new bakery in Arlington?

ANGIE *shakes her head.*

It's really good.

ANGIE. Oh cool.

FRANCES. They do these lemon cakes. I don't normally like lemon cakes but my friend Annie got one and I tried a little corner and… Yeah. Really tasty.

ANGIE *smiles and nods. Pause.*

ANGIE. Are you okay?

FRANCES. Yeah of course why?

ANGIE. On the phone you sounded…

FRANCES. Oh thanks, Angie but you don't have to – I'm not a caller!!

ANGIE. Oh okay. As long as you're alright, Frances.

FRANCES. I am

They move on to the next poster.

ANGIE *sings 'La Vie en rose', absentmindedly under her breath.*

Do you live with your boyfriend, Angie?

ANGIE. I don't have a boyfriend.

FRANCES. Oh I thought you did for some reason.

ANGIE. Nope.

FRANCES.…girlfriend?

ANGIE. No it's just me and Sandy.

…my dog.

FRANCES. Oh. That'll be… yeah.

ANGIE. And my brother comes by every week or two.

FRANCES. Oh.

Pause.

ANGIE. Is your husband a heroin addict?

FRANCES. What!? no.

ANGIE. Oh. Cool. That's really good.

FRANCES. Yeah.

ANGIE. That's really really good – cos like my mum was for a little while and so when I was born they had to like wean me off it and I just had to stay in this weird glass box for like a month and a half and apparently it made my snot really weird – like I was a really snotty baby for ages – so I think that like, while you're – while the baby is still inside you it'd be really good if you didn't have any heroin.

Pause. FRANCES *stops putting the poster up.*

FRANCES. Angie, I'm so sorry I didn't know.

ANGIE. Why are you sorry?

FRANCES *stares at* ANGIE.

She resumes putting the poster up again.

FRANCES. It was just an analogy.

ANGIE. What was it an analogy for?

FRANCES. Well he um… he's a teacher – he teaches ten-year-olds. But he's always wanted to write a novel?

ANGIE. That's cool.

FRANCES. Yeah and he – he's finished it. Finally.

ANGIE. Wow!

FRANCES. Yeah it's great.

Pause. They continue to put the posters up.

He wants to send it into space.

ANGIE. What?

FRANCES. Yeah he saw this um this advert. In a magazine. For a – for this service that is basically sending a rocket up into space with a capsule or whatever and you can pay – for a certain price – you can put something in the capsule.

ANGIE. That's so cool.

FRANCES. Do you think?

59

ANGIE. Yeah I think that's so so cool.

FRANCES. He wants to do it so that if um… if something bad happened here – were to happen here – someone somewhere might still be able to read it. Some alien species or whatever. Translate it and…

ANGIE. Wow.

FRANCES. Yeah.

Pause.

I just think that is so… *male.*

They smile at each other.

They continue in silence.

ANGIE. There's this – I used to live on a boat for a while when I was little and one time we were moored next to these mudflats? They're like these really wide stretches of barren land where rivers and tides have dumped a load of mud and sediment.

FRANCES. Mmmm.

ANGIE. And one time I was walking along the the mudflat yeah – well you kind of walk *through* it cos you sink up to your knees or so – and I found this thing buried in it. This shell thing sticking out of the surface of the mud. It was massive. Like as big as a football or something. Maybe bigger. And in my head I kind of cycled through all of the shell-based animals that I knew – trying to match it to one of them. But I couldn't. It looked different to all of them. And then I started thinking: maybe it's not from here. Like maybe it's from somewhere else. Like a different world or planet. And then, once I'd mustered up enough courage, I went over to it and I pulled it – yanked it – up out of the soil. And underneath the shell there was um this mass of tiny legs that suddenly started scuttling in the air, panicking and flailing around but mainly there were just these two massive eyes. And I was holding it up at about head height so that *its* eyes were looking straight into *my* eyes and it was like… like I was looking at something from a whole different… *place?* You know? And it was looking at me.

FRANCES. And what was it?

ANGIE. What?

FRANCES. Like what did it turn out to be?

ANGIE. Oh um. I don't know.

FRANCES. Oh.

A confused pause.

A phone rings.

ANGIE *smiles at* FRANCES *then goes to pick it up.*

ANGIE. Hello, Brightline. You're
through to someone you can talk to.

Okay.

What name would you like me to call
you?

FRANCES *watches* ANGIE, *curiously.*

FRANCES *turns to the whiteboard
and, underneath the word of the week
writes: 'CONGRATULATIONS ON
YOUR 6 MONTHS ANGIE!!!'*

JON *enters, scoffing a sandwich,
waves to everyone.*

JON. Hiya. Chat?

FRANCES. Err yes please Jon!

ANGIE. Huh. Well can you move to
somewhere where talking would be
easier? Or do you have to…

JON. How was your week?

FRANCES *is still watching* ANGIE *and doesn't reply.*

JON *sits at the computer. He reads the screen and starts typing immediately.*

Yep that sounds a lot better to me. Is it not too cold in there?

Great.

Pause.

FRANCES. Oh Jon – I wanted to talk to you about something.

JON. Mmhmm?

FRANCES. So. Hmmm.

Femi's your… cousin?

Great. What was he saying?

JON. What's up? (*Re: chat.*) This is has gone nought to sixty pretty fast / so –

Huh.

FRANCES. I've been thinking about how we talk to Joey while we're in the office.

JON. …. Okay.

FRANCES. Well I think he's at a very vulnerable time and – you know when you're that age you have all these influences and you're trying to figure out your *place* / amongst…

JON. What are you saying?

FRANCES. Okay listen. He's just starting to think really practically about the next few years and it'd be a real shame / if –

Yeah. Okay.

JOEY *enters.*

JOEY. Hiya.

Beat.

FRANCES. Hi Joey!

What are you um –

Cool trainers!

JOEY's wearing the same trainers as always. JON returns to the computer.

JOEY. Uh... thanks.

JON goes to his seat.

JON types quickly. He looks concerned.

FRANCES. Jon, you okay?

JON doesn't reply.

FRANCES goes over to sit with him.

What's going on?

Beat.

Jon?

JON. She lost her kid.

FRANCES. How?

JON. When all the fir trees went down. Playing in the woods.

FRANCES. Boy or girl?

And what do you think he meant by saying that?

Do you think there's anything else he could have meant?

Huh. Okay.

JON. Didn't say. Does it matter?

FRANCES. No. Can I?

FRANCES *scrolls up the chat.*

Her mouth moves as she reads.

*

ANGIE *is on the phone.*

FRANCES, JON *and* JOEY *are doing a training exercise and both hold finger-phones to their ears.* JON *is putting on a different accent. They are all wearing party hats and eating bits of cake.*

JOEY. No no no / I'm not trying to

ANGIE. I know you're trying to be really quiet but can I get you to talk a tiny tiny tiny bit louder for me.

JON. Well how can you possibly say that everything is / going to be

JOEY. No I said it *could* be. It *could* be.

JON. Oh it *could* be?

JOEY (*looking at* FRANCES). Yeah?

JON. And is that how I'm supposed to live, Gavin. If that is your real name. Is that how I'm supposed to get out of bed every day and make breakfast *kettle-less* every day and put the bins out every day / and errr

Thank you.

JOEY (*murmured*). who puts the bins out every day?

JON. And kiss my hus– my *wife* and my kids? Is that what I'm supposed to think when I'm reading little Rusty and Chip their bedtime stories?

FRANCES *looks down on 'kids'.*

JOEY laughs a bit.

JOEY. Rusty and Chip?

JON. Yes. After my grandmothers.

FRANCES pushes him on the shoulder.

JOEY. Uh but but but there are reasons that that it could be okay.

JON. Oh yeah?

JOEY. Yeah.

Pause. JON waits.

errrrr

JON. Okay tell me everything's gonna be okay.

JOEY. What?

JON. Just tell me everything's gonna be okay.

JOEY. ….everything's gonna be okay?

JON. What did you say? Sorry the line cut out for a second.

JOEY smiles.

JOEY. Uh… everything's gonna be okay.

JON (racing through). My daughter was playing in the wood behind our house when all the fir trees went down, the trunk landed on her ribcage, shattering all of her

Bit louder for me.

Perfecto!

Oooh what joke did you tell him?

That's a really good one.

Can I tell you one?

Knock knock

The Interrupting Cow.

MOOOOOOOO.

ANGIE laughs.

That one's great.

65

delicate little ribs into a thousand pieces, we found them scattered around her body like confetti, tell me everything's gonna be okay.

Pause.

JOEY. Uh.

FRANCES. Okay / then!

JON (*casual*). Tell me everything's gonna be okay.

JOEY. everything's gonna be okay.

JON. Say it again: everything's gonna be okay.

JOEY. Everything's gonna be okay.

JON. Everything's gonna be okay?

JOEY. Yeah.

JON. / Tell me.

FRANCES. / Jon.

JOEY. Everything's gonna be okay.

JON. Yeah?

JOEY. Everything's gonna be okay.

JON. One more time.

JOEY. Everything's gonna be okay.

ANGIE *laughs again.*

Okay okay okay one more joke then you should go back to bed and I should go talk to somebody else.

Pick the one that you like the best – I think me and you have a very similar taste in jokes. Oh and wait before you say it, can you put the card back in your dad's drawer so he can call us if he needs to?

JON. The line cut out again.

JOEY. Everything's gonna be okay. Everything's gonna be okay. Everything's gonna be / okay.

JON. Is it really? Oh I feel better.

Silence.

JOEY. I'm uh… I'm interested in why you feel the need to to impress this upon me so um… so strongly.

FRANCES. Great.

JON (*accent starting to trip up*). Because I'm not interested in treating you like a child. Because, Gavin aged twenty-seven, I am the Prophet Zephaniah sent from on high to impart wisdom in these times of darkness. And the wisdom that I have been sent to impart to you Gazza, is that the only thing that matters, when nothing matters, is having a bit of fucking credibility.

I guess what I'm telling you, Gav – Gavo – *Gagabites* – is to keep your feet on the ground.

Pause.

JOEY. Well that's very nice of you but this is a listening service and we, at Brightline, we're here for *you.* We're here to listen to your / worries.

FRANCES. Let's end it there. Really really impressive Joey. He was a tough one.

Jon, so great you gave Joey such a tricky practice run.

JON. Sorry mate, went a bit hard on you there.

FRANCES. Now the real callers will be easy peasy, right!

ANGIE *laughs.*

Okay I've got another.

Knock knock.

The Interrupting Sloth.

67

JON. / Definitely.

JOEY. / Yeah. Cool.

FRANCES. SO cool. You know you very rarely get someone quite so Hell Bent on bringing you down.

JOEY *immediately starts drawing a cartoon, his face close to the desk.*

Behind him JON and FRANCES either hold each other's gaze or they don't.

SLO-O-O-OTHHHHHHHH

ANGIE *laughs.*

*

FRANCES *and* ANGIE *are on the phone.* JON *and* JOEY *are carrying a box of files out of the room.*

FRANCES. Mmhmm.

Right.

Right. Well, why do you want to know what I'm wearing?

Okay. Some people would find that very offensive.

ANGIE. Huh. Okay that's cool.

Is there anything else you'd like to talk about?

Not cool. But you know.

Please don't –

JON *and* JOEY *re-enter with a hoover.*

You know there are numbers that you can call that are actually designed for this kind of –

JON. Can you plug me in?

JOEY *plugs it in.* JON *turns the hoover on.*

Yeah that's more what I meant.

And I'm sure you'd find them a lot more fulfilling.

Because really this number is for people who are afraid or feeling overwhelmed in some way by the current state of things. And so in some ways, in a lot of ways you're misusing the service. Unless you *are* feeling overwhelmed at all. Cos I'd be very happy to talk about that.

Huh. Okay.

Okay.

Okay if you're gonna –

Wait no no no but we're just getting to know each other!

I'm going to have to hang up the phone if you're going to persist with this but I want you to know that if you ever... if you ever do want to talk to someone... if you need reassuring or...

The line goes dead.

Goodbye.

She puts the phone down.

She shivers.

She stands.

Just gonna... go grab something from my car!

It's annoyingly loud for ANGIE and FRANCES.

FRANCES flashes JON a look. He stops hoovering. JOEY sits at his desk and starts eating his sandwich.

JON watches FRANCES – she seems uncomfortable.

A phone rings. JON answers it.

Hiya, Brightline.

JON keeps watching FRANCES, worried for her.

Mmhmm

69

She exits.

Okay.

(*As* FRANCES *exits.*) Frances are you – ?

Sorry can you you say that again for me mate?

Mmhmm.

JON *covers the receiver.*

Guys, I think I've got Merlin.

ANGIE. What?

JON. FRANCES!

JON *stands and gets as close to the door as the cord will let him.*

I think I've got Merlin!

FRANCES (*from off*). What?!

ANGIE *bounds across the room and sits/crouches next to* JON.

FRANCES *re-enters and joins them.*

JOEY. Who's Merlin?

FRANCES *puts the headset on.* ANGIE *and* JOEY *crowd round the receiver.*

JON (*to* FRANCES). I can keep going?

FRANCES. Err/rrr

JON. Sorry mate, really quickly – is there a specific name you'd like me to call you?

Pause. They wait for a response.

ANGIE *punches the air in celebration. JON and FRANCES share a smile.*

FRANCES. I thought we'd lost him.

JOEY *watches.*

JON. Great. My name's Jon. As you were, Merlin.

Yeah you have spoken to me before! Very nice to know I made an impression.

FRANCES *puts a hand on JON's shoulder. He puts his hand over hers for a moment.*

JOEY. What's going on?

ANGIE *beckons JOEY over.*

FRANCES. Okay guys we / should –

ANGIE. Merlin is this old man that calls every now and then and just monologues for about half an hour.

JON. Longer.

FRANCES. He tells these stories about his life. He spent about forty-five minutes telling me about the first time he went on a plane a couple of months ago. He'd be really detailed about the seats and the food and the view from the window.

ANGIE. Last time I spoke to him he was going on about this year he spent living in Wyoming helping out on a dairy farm. He was supposed to be there for two weeks but he like fell in love with the girl who picked up the milk so he stayed just so he could talk to her for ten minutes at 4 a.m. every day.

FRANCES. And at the end he always says Thank You and wishes you a good night.

ANGIE. He's a gentleman.

71

FRANCES. He is abusing the service though. Management hate him. We should / really

JON. Don't make me hang up.

Beat.

FRANCES. We know he's okay now. We should hang up.

They all turn to look at her, pleadingly.

JON. Give yourself a break, Frances.

Pause.

FRANCES. Okay.

JOEY. What's / so

ANGIE. Listen!

They listen.

JON. Yeah.

They listen.

Mmm

They listen. This should go on for forty-five seconds or so.

FRANCES *plucks a tissue from the box.*

ANGIE *smiles to herself.*

Maybe JON *takes* FRANCES's *hand.*

Another phone rings.

They all look at each other, nobody wanting to get it.

FRANCES. I'll / get it

JON (*firm*). Ange dya wanna…

ANGIE *grumbles but goes over to get it.*

ANGIE. Hello, Brightline. You're through to someone you can talk to.

My name's Brenda. What's yours?

Can you just speak a little clearer for me?

Sephy. That's such a pretty name. There's this dog that my dog, Sandy, really likes to play with called Sephy. She's a Lab so she's much bigger than Sandy. Kind of pushes him around to be honest. Anyway. Is there anything you'd like to talk about Sephy?

JON, FRANCES *and* JOEY *continue to listen to 'Merlin'.*

Huh.

That does sounds fun.

Yeah. Bit louder, Sephy?

And do you remember when you started feeling that way, Sephy?

JON, FRANCES *and* JOEY *snort with laughter.*

The forgetting what good news sounds like, yeah.

FRANCES *has to cover the receiver as she tries to stifle her laughter.*

Feels like, sorry, yes.

Sorry do you mind if I ask how old you are?

73

Sixteen?

Okay carry on.

Can you say that again for me just a little bit louder and a little bit clearer?

Okay I'm really struggling to hear what you're saying now. Can you really enunciate for me?

Okay well if you're having trouble, why don't we do some tongue-twisters. They're really fun. Do you know any?

My favourite was always: Betty bought a bit of butter – but the bit of butter Betty bought was bitter – so Betty bought a bit of better butter – to make the bitter butter better. Say it with me!

They glance, bemusedly at ANGIE.

Betty bought a bit of butter!

But the bit of butter Betty bought was bitter!

ANGIE *giggles*.

You're not really getting any clearer, Sephy.

So Betty bought a bit of better butter.

Sephy?

FRANCES *looks over at* ANGIE, *concerned*.

Can you hear me? Is the line bad?

Okay. Are you feeling okay?

Huh.

You sound a bit fuzzy.

Are you sure?

'Huh. It's 'to make the bitter butter better.'

Yeah. Except I'm not really hearing your Ts – you're slurring.

To make the bitter butter better.

ANGIE *stares at* FRANCES.

Sephy. Um. I really hope you don't mind me asking you this.

But have you taken any pills or tablets or…?

Because because if you have then I really need you to call an ambulance now because because I don't know where you are so…

Okay, if you just get out your mobile and dial 999 and I can stay on this line and – Sephy please keep talking to me okay? Don't stop talking otherwise I'll get worried.

Yeah that's the – bitter butter better. Ts. Good Ts!

Okay you keep going and I'll – I can say it with you.

Bitter butter better. Bitter butter better. Bitter butter better. Bitter butter better.

Bitterbutterbetterbitterbutterbetterbitterbutterbetterbitterbutterbetterbitterbutterbette rbitterbutterbetterbitterbutterbetterbitterbutterbetterbitterbutterbetterbitterbutterbett erbitterbutterbetterbitterbutterbetterbitterbutterbetterbitterbutterbetterbitterbutterbet terbitterbutterbetterbitterbutterbetterbitterbutterbetterbitterbutterbetterbitterbutterbe tterbitterbutterbetterbitterbutterbetterbitterbutterbetterbitterbutterbetterbitterbutterb etterbitterbutterbetterbitterbutterbetterbitterbutterbetterbitterbutterbetterbitterbutter betterbitterbutterbetter.

Silence.

JON *and* JOEY *are now looking at* ANGIE *as well.*

FRANCES *goes to sit next to* ANGIE. *She puts her headset on.*

FRANCES (*steely*). Angie.

FRANCES *takes the phone.*

FRANCES. Sephy, can you tap the phone to let me know that you're still there?

Pause.

If you're still there can you tap it for me?

Beat.

FRANCES *turns to* ANGIE *and hugs her tight.*

ANGIE *takes the phone back and presses it to her ear.*

Long silence.

FRANCES *pulls away.*

Ange, you're gonna have to put the phone down.

Pause.

Angie.

I need you to put the phone down now.

ANGIE. What happens?

FRANCES. I don't know. I don't know what happens.

Someone will find her. Over the next few days or so.

But I need you to put the phone down.

Now, Angie.

Please.

Please.

Please.

Pause.

FRANCES presses the hang-up button on the desktop phone console. The line goes dead.

ANGIE stares at her in horror.

FRANCES stares at the floor.

ANGIE. Why.

Another phone rings. Neither FRANCES nor ANGIE seem to register it. They remain statue-still. FRANCES doesn't answer her. It continues to ring.

Why.

FRANCES says nothing.

JOEY *answers it.*

JOEY. Hello.

Hi Nish. Yeah mmhmm.

When did – um – how did it start?

Blackout.

Week Four

On the whiteboard is written: 'WORD OF THE WEEK – COMMUNICATION!!!'

One of the desks has collapsed and all of the files, etc., resting on it have spilled on to the floor. The posters have fallen off the wall again. It's a tip.

JOEY and JON are sat there. Maybe JON's on a chair and JOEY's on the edge of a desk.

JON is holding a lighter underneath a mug, trying to warm its contents with the flame.

JOEY. Yeah I thought it was like… really creepy.

JON. Yeah I see that.

JOEY. I thought a bat was gonna fly out at me or something you know. Or like a ton of bats. Like thirty or forty bats.

JON. Yeah I guess it's dark and kind of dusty.

JOEY. So dusty. You know when you go into a place and it's scary so you squeeze your eyes closed really tight for a second (*Does so.*) then you open them and kind of plan your escape route? Like you go: Oh I'd jump off there and climb down that pipe thing and pivot on to that tree.

JON. Do you do that?

JOEY. Uh / well

JON. Squeeze your eyes shut and plan an escape route.

JOEY. I dunno. Sometimes.

If there are bats.

Pause. JON grimaces in pain and rubs his lower back.

But it's like crazy creaky up there now. I thought I was gonna fall right through the floorboards into the canteen.

JON. Yeah.

JOEY. Did you actually have… *sex* up there?

JON. I didn't. But people did.

JOEY. Whoa.

I'd be all in my head about falling through. It'd totally put me off my game.

Beat.

JON. Your game?

JOEY. …yeah.

Pause.

Oh and I told a load of people about Thornburg. About what you said. That he's not a legend or anything. There was no dungeon.

JON. Oh yeah?

JOEY. Yeah.

JON. What did they say?

JOEY. They thought it was funny. And amazing that I met a guy that was there then. But they still think he probably did have a dungeon.

JON. Classic.

JOEY. I guess it's more fun to believe it.

JON. Yeah.

Pause. He takes a sip of the coffee, grimaces and puts it down.

God I miss kettles.

JOEY. Yeah. I miss pedal boats.

I never went on one. Just thought it looked fun.

JON. They were fun.

JOEY *laughs*.

Been down to West Rowe recently?

JOEY. No.

JON. I took Andy for a drive down there at the weekend.

They've got mould growing on their skin. It's in their eyelids. And in their dimples when they smile.

It's on all the buildings too. Just these big fuzzy purple-green blotches right there in the brick.

JOEY *gags*.

Sorry.

JOEY. It's okay.

Pause.

Sounds romantic.

JON *starts to laugh*. JOEY *smiles*.

JON. Yeah.

JON *gets up and tries to stretch out his back.*

What you doing?

JON. My back is killing me.

JOEY. What about your wonder mattress that saves your life on a daily basis?

JON. Feels like one of those – what are those trucks that roll out cement called? The ones with like a metal barrel for a wheel?

JOEY. …I think they're just called roller trucks.

JON. Feels like one of them has just really gone to town on my whole spinal situation.

He keeps stretching. He groans.

This is my apocalypse.

JOEY *smiles.*

Pause.

JOEY. It's weird. I went up there between classes – I had this free period after DT that nobody else really has because only me and this girl Lorraine take DT. And I thought that'd be a good time to sneak up there because it'd be pretty quiet. You know, everyone would be in lessons. And when I was there, after I got over the bat thing and the escape-plan thing, I was sitting in the corner thinking about you coming up here when you were my age. And I had this like – I don't think I'm a very imaginative person or anything – but I kind of suddenly had this really vivid image of a seventeen-year-old you climbing up that ladder. Putting your knee on the floorboards to push yourself up. And your hand wiping the dust from the patch you were gonna sit in.

He wipes his hand along the desk, imitating it.

Just that little… motion. Really clearly. And it was kind of like – even though it was years ago – it was like there was this line being drawn in front of my eyes.

Silence.

81

JON. I presume Lorraine wasn't also there.

JOEY. No. Lorraine always stays in the DT room to work on this chest of drawers she's making.

JON. Good on Lorraine.

JOEY. Lorraine's really good with pine.

JON smiles.

JON. Are you gonna be like a carpenter when you grow up? Wear overalls wherever you go and have like a pencil behind each ear so you're always ready to… *carpent.*

JOEY laughs.

JOEY. Yeah. I dunno. I don't find it useful to think too far ahead.

Pause. They hold eye contact.

JON. Do you um – when you get home do you like *tell* your – you live with your mum and dad right?

JOEY. Just my mum.

JON. Oh. Your dad…?

JOEY. He lives in the flat below us.

JON. What?

JOEY. Yeah. It's weird. But we don't really – you know, I don't really talk to him. Or see him.

JON. Oh.

JOEY. But sometimes – he's a piano teacher mainly but he's one of those people that can just pick up an instrument and be amazing at it straight away. It's really annoying!

But yeah sometimes I can hear him playing through the floor. So I know he's there I guess.

Sorry you were gonna ask me something?

JON. Oh. No.

JOEY. No I wanna / know!

JON. It doesn't matter.

JOEY. Tell me.

Pause.

JON. Could you crack my back?

JOEY. Uh.

JON. You don't have to. / If it's weird.

JOEY. Yeah? I mean I don't know how but...

JON. Oh it's easy you just kind of lift me um – here let me show you.

JON beckons JOEY up. He turns him around.

Okay so cross your arms over your chest. And...

JOEY does so. JON stands behind JOEY, wraps his arms around him and, leaning back, lifts him into the air.

JOEY's back cracks. He puts him back down and releases him. JOEY shakes it off.

JOEY. Whoa.

JON. Feel better?

JOEY. Yeah. I didn't know you could crack a back.

JON. You can crack a back.

84

JOEY *turns* JON *round.*

JON *crosses his arms over his chest.*

JOEY *lifts him into the air.*

He struggles – JON*'s a lot bigger and heavier than him.*

No crack.

He puts him back down.

But he doesn't let go.

JOEY. Did it…?

JON. Oh. No. Don't worry I'll just… suffer on.

They stand there for a moment, JOEY *holding* JON*.* JON*'s arms remain awkwardly crossed over his chest. It's somewhere between romance and friendship. Support, more than anything else. Maybe* JON *closes his eyes.*

Then JOEY *pulls away.*

Pause. They smile at each other.

FRANCES *enters.*

FRANCES. So sorry I'm late guys. I had a scan and the waiting time was a bit longer than me and Harry were expecting it to be and he had a meeting he had to go to and take the car and that meant that I had to take a couple of buses so…

Beat.

Great to see you guys.

JON. Boy or girl?

FRANCES. We want it to be a surprise.

JON. Oh come on you definitely know! I won't / tell Harry.

FRANCES. So Angie's not coming in today. Her dog is sick. It – *he* – has been throwing up and diarrhoea-ing all over her flat so she doesn't want to leave the poor guy.

JON and JOEY exchange a glance.

JOEY. Is she okay?

FRANCES. Angie? Yeah! She's fine – it's just her – just the dog must have eaten something. Jon, you look tired.

JON. Thanks.

FRANCES. I don't mean that / in a

JON. It's okay.

FRANCES. Have you been getting enough sleep?

JON. I guess not.

FRANCES. Oh dear. It's uh… sleep's really important.

JON *(not entirely sardonically).* Thanks for your concern, Frances.

FRANCES. Joey! *(Roots around in her bag.)* Your mum sent me over the first draft of your personal statement / so I've printed it off and made

JOEY *(glancing at* JON, *mortified).* What!? Why did she do that?

FRANCES. Well you hadn't sent it over yet so I just dropped her a text / and

JOEY. Err well it was just / something I had to

FRANCES. Anyway I've printed it off and made a few annotations. / Just little grammar and spelling suggestions really.

JOEY. It was just something I had to do for homework. I didn't put a lot of effort in or anything.

85

FRANCES. I think it's really brilliant, Joey. It actually brought a little tear to my eye!

JOEY. ....really?

FRANCES. Mmhmm.

JON. Wow!

FRANCES holds the piece of paper out to JOEY. He doesn't take it.

FRANCES. We can go through it together later.

Pause.

JOEY grabs the paper from her and sits down. Maybe he hides it under a load of other papers on his desk. He turns away from both of them.

JON snorts with laughter, turns around and busies himself with papers.

I actually have to talk to you guys about something.

JON. What's up?

FRANCES. Well I spoke to Helen at regional head office. And basically it seems as though a few of our bigger donors have decided to pull their investment.

JON. This has been happening for ages though right?

FRANCES. Yeah. But it seems to have become fairly serious.

JON. Are they shutting us down?

FRANCES. No! No they're not shutting us down. They are shutting a couple of branches down but not ours! So well done us! Great news!

JOEY. ....cool?

JON. That's cos nobody wants this shitty piece of real estate anyway. Our rent must just about balance the landlord's tax on it right? They may as well call it a wash / rather than

FRANCES. Anyway. Because of all that, Helen and I came up with a few changes to our erm our practice that should help us get a better lay of the land. And we're gonna be the first branch to try them out!

JOEY. / ...Okay?

JON. / What does that mean?

FRANCES. It's not a big deal or anything but what we're gonna do – at the end of the phone call, whenever you sense the caller is about to hang up – all we're gonna do is ask them really quickly and simply if they've found the service useful or not. So hopefully we'll get a better read on how um – you know / how...

JON. Are you kidding?

FRANCES. Yeah and then, if they are *forthcoming* with their response, there's like a small list of follow-up questions.

JON. Is this straight out of your MA groups?

FRANCES. Not strictly, no. I just think it could be a really great way of showing the world that we're doing really good work, that we're making a real, positive impact on people.

JON. That's the dumbest thing I've ever heard.

FRANCES. Well I'm really excited about it.

JOEY. It does sound a bit dumb, Frances.

JON. 'I'm just afraid that I'm gonna die and that everyone I know is gonna die and all of our lives rendered entirely meaningless.'

'Okay, Karen, can I just get you to rate your experience today out of five.'

FRANCES. I think it'll be really good to know what people think of the service. Really good to hear how much / it's appreciated.

JON. They were gonna shut us down too weren't they? You're literally *bribing* Helen with the prospect of fresh publicity / material!

87

FRANCES. Jon. Stop.

Pause.

Anyway it's just something that we're gonna have to throw ourselves into for a little while, okay? Just until things get back on track, money-wise.

Murmurs of compliance.

I'll give Angie a call and talk it through with her before next week.

JOEY. Why are they pulling out? The donors.

JON scoffs, turns away and tries to fix one of the broken desks.

FRANCES. We don't know why they pulled out, Joey. They didn't say. So all we can do in this situation is remember that – that what we are doing is important and useful and good because – because people need to know that stuff is gonna work out.

Pause.

JOEY (*to* FRANCES, *uncertainly*). Err err – (*Motions to* JON.) stuff is gonna / work out, Frances.

JON. stuff's gonna work out, Frances.

Beat.

FRANCES. No not me, Joey – I don't / to be – it's them that

A phone rings. They look at it.

FRANCES *takes a deep breath and answers it.*

Hello Brightline, you're through to someone you can talk to.

Yep you've got the right number. What would you like to talk about today?

Absolutely. That sounds like a great thing to talk about.

JON and JOEY exchange a weary glance. JOEY goes to help JON mend the desk.

Well, try for me, okay? Please.

Another phone rings. JOEY picks it up.

Yep yep that's great.

No! You're doing so –

The phone goes dead.

FRANCES stands up, looking for something to do.

JON sets the desk up and it falls down again. He groans.

JON. Does anyone have a cigarette?

FRANCES. I thought you quit.

JON. I did yeah. Don't tell Andy.

FRANCES. Very bad for you, you know.

JON. Oh I do.

FRANCES. I. Think. We. Need. Some. Doughnuts!

FRANCES exits.

JON notices when JOEY says 'Andy'.

JOEY. Hello Brightline, you're through to someone you can talk to.

Mmhmm okay.

Yeah yeah yeah. That's – that's what this is for really.

Can I just ask – you don't have to answer this now but when you've finished talking can you uh – can you just stay on the line for a tiny bit while I ask you some quick questions but YOU DON'T HAVE TO ANSWER NOW! Let's just – yeah you tell me the thing – forget I said that – let's just start again.

Hi. Yeah.

Errrr my name is…

Andy.

What name can I call you?

Oh wow. That's weird. That's never happened to me before.

Not that long but still.

Yeah – you too, Andy.

Is there anything you'd like to talk to me about?

Okay.

He dismisses it and sits down at a desk, centre-stage.

Take your time.

First time's always weird.

JON picks up JOEY's lunchbox and looks at the cartoon on the front.

Where are you calling me from?

JON (to JOEY). That's cool.

Is anyone there with you?

JOEY smiles at him.

Why are you moving house?

JON looks up at JOEY. He watches the conversation from now on. The focus should be on him.

Oh that's just near where my school is.

Was. Sorry. I'm too old for school now. Obviously.

Yeah. Anyway you were saying about the fresh-start thing.

A fresh start from what?

Pause.

Andy, you still there?

That's okay.

It's okay.

JON is leaning forward, hanging on JOEY's next words.

No – I don't think you're being confrontational at all! Especially compared to – like sometimes we get some pretty scary…

But I totally get that it's weird talking to someone you don't even fucking know.

Yeah exactly. Uh.

Beat.

Dya wanna just take a moment to... I'll just be quiet and you can be quiet and then we can either keep going or not?

Andy?

Cool.

Silence. JOEY holds the phone to his ear.

JOEY smiles at JON politely. Unknowingly.

Okay?

Great.

What would you like to talk about?

Okay what's your husband's name?

Sorry you don't have to –

JOEY realises who he's speaking to. He glances at JON.

FRANCES *enters with doughnuts.*

FRANCES. Doughnut time!

A phone goes off.

Jon can you?

JON *doesn't even register.* FRANCES *answers it.*

Hello! Brightline here. You're through to someone you can talk to.

Mmhmm

JON *stares at him.*

Pause. JOEY thinks. He goes to put the phone down, then doesn't.

JOEY turns away from JON slightly.

Um. Sorry, Andy, I lost you for a second.

    Okay. Go grab yourself a glass of water.

Uh. How long have you been together? Did you say that already?

Right yeah.

    Can you tap the phone to let me know you're there?

    Great. Thank you. Yeah your voice does sound a lot better now – less hoarse!

Yeah. But uh that makes sense – it's the opposites-attract thing right?

What so he *enjoys* making you feel like –

Yeah hope!– like the glass is half-empty yeah.

JOEY steals a glance at JON.

JON *is open-mouthed.*

Well uh... you know that can be useful sometimes can't it? It's good to be practical. And have some uh... like realistic expectation.

    You can take your time. There's no rush.

(Quietly.) Hang up the phone.

Credibility! Yeah that was the word I was…

Okay.

No I'm not saying that's not still… difficult.

Pause. JOEY doesn't look at JON.

JOEY gulps.

Do you think he *wants* you to be as miserable as he is?

(*Slightly louder.*) Hang up the phone.

Like when he makes that sound and that face he's not trying to –

(*Slightly louder again.*) Hang up the phone.

He sounds like a um – you know – like a really good guy who's just… yeah.

JON turns away, giving up.

Oh right okay. Well it's been really good to talk to you, Andy. From one

Hello?

By the way, are you finding this call useful today?

Are you still there?

The line goes dead.

Just gonna pop to the loo.

FRANCES exits.

Andy to the other! So okay if you could just rate your experience today out of five that would be –

The phone goes dead.

A horrible silence.

JON *stands and walks towards the door.*

JOEY. Jon / uh

As JON *passes* JOEY's *desk he snatches the personal statement that* FRANCES *printed off.*

Whoa. Uh. Jon that's um…

JON. I thought I could give you some notes?

JOEY. That's just a stupid – / I had to do it for school – it's not

JON. Yeah I thought you didn't like to think too far ahead.

JOEY. I don't – Like I don't wanna go / or anything.

JON. Read it to me.

JOEY. Jon –

JON. Read it to me. Go on.

Beat.

Go on. I wanna hear it.

JOEY *(reading aloud)*. I've always been very good at drawing cartoons since I was able to manipulate my fingers into the grip of a pencil. My mum and dad used to have to rip the HB Graphite drawing implement out of my tiny hands when it was

JON. Louder.

time to go to bed or to have a bath or to go on an errand. And this only blossomed as I grew, both in age and in size. (*Aside*.) That sounded kinda poetic-y in my head.

JON *says nothing.*

JOEY (*continuing*). I think it's kind of interesting that characters in comics don't grow up. The whole world can change in a comic: it can go back in time and it can enter New Ages that are unlike all the ages we know and love. And they'll still be there wearing the same outfits and saying the same catchphrases and making the same dumb mistakes. It's like time happens all around them. But not inside them. Just because they're made out of lines instead of atoms. They never have to think about who they're going to become and therefore the future doesn't seem scary to them. Like it does to us.

FRANCES *enters*.

FRANCES. Oh great!

Pause.

FRANCES. Love that bit at the end.

JON. I think that's fucking brilliant mate.

FRANCES. Isn't it just!

Beat.

JOEY. thanks.

JON. I think you're gonna get in.

JOEY. thanks

JON. I think you've got a long sparkling life ahead of you, mate.

JOEY. thanks.

Pause.

95

FRANCES. So lovely that you're showing an interest, Jon.

JON. Mmhmm.

JOEY. (*To* JON.) Why d'you even come here?

Pause.

JON. (*To* JOEY.) Hey stick the kettle on would you?

JON *pushes past* FRANCES *and exits.*

Pause. JOEY *turns away from* FRANCES.

FRANCES. What's going on?

JOEY *nods.*

FRANCES *follows* JON *off.*

JOEY *sits there, alone.*

We hear the muffled sound of JON *and* FRANCES *arguing outside.*

JOEY *squeezes his eyes closed really tight.*

He opens them and looks around.

He squeezes his eyes closed again. Tighter than ever.

He opens them.

*

A briefing session – they sit facing each other.

Pause.

FRANCES. Nobody wants to leave anything here?

Nothing.

Nobody wants to leave anything here.

Nothing.

Okay you know what I'd quite like to do – just because I think occasionally, at points tonight the mood has been maybe a bit low? I'd like to play a game. I'd like to play a game just to make sure that we're hitting the street with the same positive energy that we usually do!

FRANCES *stands and starts rooting around in all the drawers. She pulls out the deflated beach ball and starts blowing it up frantically.*

JON. Oh god Frances are you serious?

JOEY. I really don't want to play a game.

JON. I think it's a bad idea.

JOEY. I think a game is the worst thing that could possibly happen.

FRANCES. Okay okay sorry errr well let's just let's just – we could dance – put on a song and dance

JOEY. OH MY GOD.

FRANCES. Or we could sing – let's sing um –

JOEY. / No please no.

JON. / Have you lost your…

FRANCES. I don't think any of us should leave here until we're feeling better.

JON. Frances you need / to stop.

FRANCES. Jon you could play us a song on your trombone! / YES! You could play us a song!

JON. WHAT. Are you completely out of your – / you've fully lost it

FRANCES. YES that's it that's it! Cos we'll be proud of you of all the work that you've been – yes I do think that – I do – YEP YEP YEP. I think that will make all of us – put in perspective for everyone what has been going on. I think it's perfect to be honest, Jon.

YAY! Isn't that great Joey? Isn't that just a perfect end to the night. To to to see how much WORK and EFFORT and HOPE and GOOD WILL Jon has poured into learning to play the trombone! Right Joey!

I think that would be great I think that would be lovely and if you want me to I will communicate that to head office.

JON. You think me playing a fucking – that's gonna make everyone feel chirpy? – You think that is gonna magically evaporate – oh you do – you do – you do think everything is just going to melt away at the sound of my pathetic, shitty – you do – you – OKAY I'LL DO IT! I'M GONNA PLAY THE TROMBONE. (*Moves to the corner and starts unzipping his trombone case.*) IT'S 4 A.M. AND I'M GONNA PLAY THE TROMBONE BECAUSE THAT IS THE ANSWER WE HAVE BEEN LOOKING FOR. WE SHOULD JUST PLAY TROMBONE STRAIGHT INTO THE PHONES. THAT WOULD SOLVE EVERYTHING RIGHT? THE DONORS WILL STOP PULLING OUT, THE TREES WILL COME BACK, THE AIR WILL BE CLEAN, THE KETTLES WILL BOIL

JON has got his trombone out of its case, lifts it to his lips and launches into 'Ode to Joy'.

He is terrible at it and fluffs several notes. The tune is only just about recognisable.

He plays the melody slowly, taking ages to get from note to note. It's a marathon.

What is normally a forty-five-second piece should be double that.

By the time he starts the second phrase his shoulders have begun to shake a bit.

By the end it's pretty horrible to watch.

He finishes. Maybe he fluffs the last note.

Silence.

Blackout.

Week Five

The lights don't come up.

FRANCES enters in darkness. There is an inch or two of water covering the entire floor. FRANCES's shoes squelch with each step.

She fiddles with the light switch.

Nothing.

FRANCES. Oh crap.

FRANCES goes over to one of the phone consoles. She dials a number, puts the phone to her ear.

It rings.

Hi Harry, it's me. Sorry I just needed to check the phones were working here and yours was the number I…

Yeah all the lights have gone down.

Thanks.

Um yeah.

Yes obviously I know that.

Yeah.

Thank you for saying that.

Listen I can't have this conversation here so – you're not supposed to take personal calls on…

Okay. Um. If we're trying to be totally honest with each other. Yeah. I've known for a while. I know you wanted it to be a surprise. But I just had to know what I'm about to bring into the world. I'm sorry I didn't say anything. I didn't want to ruin it for you.

Pause.

Are you sure?

Okay.

Um

Okay can you do me a favour though? Just for the – just for the duration of this phone call can you just not get like you were about to.

Because… because I think you might.

But if, for now you could just pretend to be… you know, I'd really appreciate it.

And it's okay if you do it after – just not when we're still – when there's this cord connecting…

Okay.

It's twins!

Yeah.

A boy and a girl.

Pause. FRANCES *takes some deep breaths.*

Okay I need to go and sort out these lights.

Bye. Thanks, Harry.

FRANCES *hangs up the phone and leans on the table for a moment.*

She then goes to riffle round a few drawers.

This should take a while.

She checks every drawer in the room.

When she is next to the radio, she turns it on. 'Suzanne' by Leonard Cohen plays quietly.

FRANCES exits and walks down the corridor to the office.

The stage is empty for about twenty seconds. We listen to the song. And the sound of torrential rain from outside. Maybe some seeps round the corner of the cardboard-covered window and trickles down the wall.

Eventually FRANCES returns carrying an armload of candles.

She slowly goes around the room, placing and then lighting each of the candles.

There should probably be about fifteen lit candles? The rest of the play is conducted by candlelight.

The whiteboard reads: 'WORD OF THE WEEK – O TI SM !'

'THE LIGHTS AREN'T WORKING!!!!'

FRANCES smiles at the words on the whiteboard.

JOEY enters. He registers the candles.

Hey Joey!

JOEY. What's…?

FRANCES. We're having a little problem with the lights.

JOEY. Oh. But the phones…

FRANCES. Phones are all good.

Pause. JOEY goes to dump his stuff by his desk. FRANCES keeps lighting the candles. Her voice catches in her throat when she speaks.

Hey Joe, did you uh…

Did you fix those little typos and grammar things in your personal statement?

Pause.

JOEY. Uh. Well. I actually told my teacher that I'm not gonna apply at all this year. So uh… he said that there wasn't much point me finishing off the statement. In that case.

FRANCES. Oh.

JOEY. Yeah. But uh… thanks for the, you know, all the help and stuff.

Beat.

FRANCES. No problem.

JOEY. I really appreciate it.

FRANCES *smiles at him.*

FRANCES. Joey, if I give you some money could you run out and get us some doughnuts?

JOEY. Yeah sure.

FRANCES. You wouldn't mind? I just want to finish setting up here.

JOEY. Sure.

She roots around for some money in her bag. JOEY watches her. She finds it. We hear a siren, loud, passing outside.

FRANCES. Hurray!

She hands it over. JOEY hesitates then exits.

103

A phone rings.

Hello, Brightline. You're through to someone you can talk to.

My name is Emily, what can I call you?

Pause. FRANCES *sighs.*

I'm wearing a pretty standard pair of jeans and a shirt.

It's not very interesting or... *sexy*

I'm also seven months pregnant by the way if that...?

Nope. Okay.

FRANCES *looks around – nobody there.*

Why are you doing this?

Why can't you just be... polite?

Not kind. Caring. Just polite.

I don't understand it.

So I'm really supposed to stay on the line for a while here. Just so that if, at any point in the future, you *are* feeling like you actually need someone to talk to – if you're scared or worried or overwhelmed – you'll know that we're here for that.

Beat.

But I want you to never call this number again.

She hangs up.

FRANCES *crouches down and puts her hands over her ears.*

Pause.

JON *enters. He doesn't have his trombone. He hangs his gas mask up.*

JON. Are we having a vigil?

FRANCES *stands up.*

FRANCES. The lights are down.

JON. Ah.

He steps into the room with a splash.

Should've brought my wellies.

FRANCES *doesn't reply.*

How was your week?

FRANCES. It was okay.

JON. Whoa.

FRANCES. What?

JON. I've just… nothing.

JON *starts helping* FRANCES *fix up the room. Either he lights more candles or he tries to right the half-collapsed table.*

FRANCES. How was your week?

JON. I went camping.

FRANCES. What?

JON. I went camping.

FRANCES. With Andy?

JON. Nope.

FRANCES. On your own?

JON. Yep.

FRANCES. I didn't know people still did that.

JON. I don't think they do really.

FRANCES. Did you have to wear your mask the whole time?

JON. Yep. It was incredibly inconvenient.

Did you know anyone?

FRANCES. What? Oh.

Um. Yeah. Guy I went to uni with.

JON. I'm sorry.

FRANCES. It's okay. We'd kinda lost touch. He went out with one of my best friends and when they broke up we had to do the side-picking thing, you know.

JON. Yeah.

I'm sorry though.

FRANCES. It's okay.

You?

JON. A few people yeah.

FRANCES. I'm sorry.

Pause.

Why did you go camping?

JON. Don't know really.

It was an Impulse Decision.

FRANCES. That's nice.

JON. And I thought trying something new wouldn't actually be... you know.

FRANCES. The end of the world?

JON. Yeah.

A warmer pause. They tidy on in silence.

Angie's not coming back is she.

FRANCES *shrugs*.

Pause.

I really wanna ask you something but it's gonna sound really aggressive and judgemental and I don't want it to sound that way.

FRANCES. Okay.

JON. It's gonna be pretty horrible.

FRANCES. I think we're all quite used to hearing horrible things.

JON. No but this is gonna sound like proper fucking knife in / the back –

FRANCES. What / is it?

107

JON. Blood pouring out everywhere. You gasping / for breath.

FRANCES. Jon. What.

JON. Can you just close your eyes when I say it?

FRANCES. Uh.

JON. You've just always got those stupid headlight-beamy things glaring / up at

FRANCES. Is this the horrible thing?

JON. No.

Pause.

FRANCES. Okay.

FRANCES *closes her eyes.*

Lay it on me.

Pause.

JON. It's just been going round my head for a few months. In some form or other I guess.

Cos I don't understand. And, for some reason, I think if I did, everything would be a lot clearer. Maybe.

FRANCES. Jon.

JON. Do you – ARGH

Do you regret getting pregnant?

FRANCES *opens her eyes.* JON *looks away.*

FRANCES. No.

JON. Okay.

Silence.

Eventually JON resumes tidying – maybe he heaves the collapsed table over to the side of the room and props it against the wall as he talks. Only two of the desks are fixable. They push them together at the front of the room.

I've been living in um – we're moving house at the moment. Feels like we've been doing it forever. But Andy's moved into the new one. With all our stuff. And I've just stayed back at ours. I'm kind of squatting. Sleeping on a bedsheet on top of this lovely soft bit of floorboard.

And I keep trying to stop dragging him…

I keep trying to be more… present or open or whatever.

Joyful.

Joyful.

I first started calling this place about two years ago. A couple of times a week maybe. Spoke to you a lot. This was when me and Andy first started arguing about it. Didn't help at all. Didn't make me feel any more… you know.

So I thought that if I had to pretend enough. To these fuckers (*Motions to phones.*) I might get better?

Because right now.

I'm just sucking it out of him you know?

I'm just sucking it out.

JON makes a long sucking sound with his mouth.

Silence.

FRANCES *turns to* JON.

110

FRANCES. Sometimes.

Not today.

But sometimes.

Pause. They hold each other's gaze.

FRANCES feels the babies kicking.

She puts her hands on her stomach.

JON walks over and puts his hands on her stomach to feel the babies kick.

JON. That's fucking weird.

FRANCES smiles at him.

JOEY enters.

JOEY. So they didn't – oh hi.

JON. Hiya.

Beat

JOEY. They didn't have any doughnuts left. The shop's basically empty actually. Uh. So I just got us some rice cakes and a jar of peanut butter.

A phone rings. JON sits and answers.

FRANCES. That's great, Joey. I'll get us some paper plates.

FRANCES exits.

JOEY moves the chairs so that they're all gathered around the one remaining desk.

He gets out his lunchbox and starts eating his sandwich.

JON. Hello Brightline, how can I help?

Errr. So –

Excuse me –

Hiya love. Sorry I think you've got the wrong number.

Another phone rings. JOEY answers it.

JOEY. Hello Brightline, you're through to someone you can talk to.

No there's no Polly here sorry.

Hello?

Can you tap the phone so I know you're still there?

No I'm gonna struggle to pass a message on – this is actually a call centre not a

Great, thanks. Well just to let you know. You can just talk about anything you want to and I'll just have a listen really. That's how it works. Is this your first time?

Yeah.

Hello?

Cheers. Yeah.

Can you tap the phone again?

JON *hangs up the phone.*

Okay. Great. Well I'm just gonna wait for you to start then? Whenever you feel comfortable. Take your time.

He watches JOEY *for a while – impressed.*

Silence.

JOEY *covers the receiver.*

JON *starts sorting some papers, trying to make space on the desk.*

Oh Jon, by the way. Is your husband – uh – is he like… Scandinavian?

JON. What?

JOEY. Oh just cos last week at one point I got this call from this guy who said his name was Andy – which is your husband's name right? And uh he was talking about moving house and stuff so I thought – you know – there's a chance it could be…? BUT he had this really really strong unmistakable Scandinavian accent so unless your husband is from one of the Scandinavian countries, it, like a-hundred-per-cent, no-doubt-about-it wasn't him.

Pause.

JON. What does a Scandinavian accent sound like?

JOEY. Oh it's kind of sing-songy?

JON. Sing-songy?

JOEY. Yeah definitely a kind of musicality to it.

JON. Right.

JOEY. A lightness maybe?

JON. Oh yeah?

JOEY. Yeah. (*Into phone.*) Hi! Yeah I'm still here. Sorry.

Yeah whatever you want.

Okay you don't have to. That's cool too.

Uh yeah whenever you want.

Can I just quickly ask if this call has been helpful for –

The line goes dead. JOEY *puts the phone down.*

(*To* JON.) What?

JON. You handled that well.

JOEY. Thanks

JON. That was a nice story.

JOEY. What story? Oh no that's um… that's real. That really happened.

So your… he's not…

Scandinavian?

FRANCES *re-enters carrying three cups of water and some paper plates. She walks over slowly trying not to spill the water.*

Pause.

JON. You're seventeen.

JOEY. …yeah.

Pause.

JON. Must've been a different guy.

Pause.

ANGIE *appears in the doorway.*

FRANCES. Angie.

ANGIE. Hi.

What happened to the…?

FRANCES. They're um… They're boken.

ANGIE. Okay. Do the phones still…

FRANCES. Yep.

ANGIE. Okay.

FRANCES. How's your dog?

ANGIE. Oh uh. Yeah. He's doing alright. Thanks

Pause. ANGIE *hesitates then goes to sit down at the desk. The four of them look strangely close together, huddled round the last remaining desk.*

FRANCES. Angie you missed Jon playing us his trombone last week.

FRANCES *unpacks the shopping on to the table.*

113

ANGIE. Oh no really?

FRANCES. Yeah.

He's really getting good! And that was the first time you'd performed in public?

JON *nods*.

'A WORLD PREMIERE OF JON'

You know, I don't know your last name.

How do I not know your last name?

JON. I don't really tell people my last name.

JOEY. What?

JON. I try to keep it off registers and stuff.

FRANCES. Why?

JOEY. What is it?

Beat.

JON. It's Lennon.

FRANCES. What.

JON. Yeah.

JOEY. Your name is John Lennon.

JON. Yeah. I don't have an 'H' in Jon. But yeah.

JOEY. well that's fucking ridiculous.

JON. I know.

JOEY. You're like the least suitable person for that name.

JON. Yep.

FRANCES. John Lennon played in my office last week.

ANGIE's phone rings.

She stares at it. The others watch her.

She waits.

She waits.

FRANCES leans forward and holds ANGIE's hand.

She waits.

JON goes to pick up ANGIE's phone instead.

ANGIE. no.

ANGIE takes a deep breath and picks it up.

Hello?

Yes this is Brightline. You've got the right number.

Huh. Okay. Well. You should tell me about that.

ANGIE gives FRANCES a gratified look and FRANCES lets go of her hand.

JON's phone rings.

JON. Hello Brightline, you're through to someone you can talk to.

Huh. Okay.

Well from the sounds of it that's definitely true.

Huh. Mmhmm.

Huh.

But isn't that different to saying she's draining the hope out of you?

No of course not. I s'pose I'm just trying to get some context.

Huh.

FRANCES *picks up* JOEY's *lunchbox*.

FRANCES. What's on your lunchbox?

JOEY. It's a Charlie Brown comic. My mum got it me.

FRANCES *tries to read it but it's too dark. She shrugs.*

FRANCES. Can't read it.

JOEY. Um. So it's night and Linus – he's one of the characters – he lights a candle and goes (*Pompous voice.*) 'I have heard that it is always better to light a candle than to curse the darkness' and then Lucy – one of the other characters – is just outside shouting 'YOU STUPID DARKNESS!' into the sky. In like... comic sans.

JOEY's *phone rings.*

Hello, Brightline. You're through to someone you can talk to.

Yep sure.

Okay.

Great. Go ahead.

Mhmm.

Yep I get that.

Alright that's uh – Sorry yeah.

Okay can you just walk me through

Yeah! Those things can feel so so so huge and then…

An example? Well we're not really supposed to talk about ourselves here.

FRANCES *smiles at* ANGIE – *granting her permission.*

But um. If you're asking.
This thing happened to me a couple of weeks ago and I've been thinking about it quite a lot I s'pose.

FRANCES *looks around at the candles.*

And at JOEY, JON *and* ANGIE. *Still going.*

Well uh – what do you think she'd say if you knew she felt that way.

Bob Dylan's 'Shelter from the Storm' is playing quietly over the radio.
FRANCES *wipes a tear from her eye.*

FRANCES. Who wants a peanut-butter rice cake?

ANGIE *pumps both fists in the air.*

JOEY. Yes please!
FRANCES *passes round the food.*

Very slowly the sound of the rain outside begins to swell. An echoey siren. The song from the radio fades up to the theatre speakers.

Okay and how would that feel?

that reasoning one more time.
Just interested in why you've put those things together.

Yeah see I think you're giving yourself a tough time there, mate.

Alright I see that yeah. That makes sense.

Yeah exactly. It's a balance.

(*To* FRANCES.) Can I get more peanut butter on mine? Really lather it on.

(*To phone.*) Listen I hate to do this but I have to ask you for some feedback on your calling experience today.
Yeah.

And sometimes, a lot of the time actually, it feels like this big explosion in my head. That wipes out everything else. This kinda barren, dead landscape, you know?

Mmhmm yeah.

But then other times it feels like just a thing that happened.

That's great.

And I don't really have any control over that yet. But I'm trying.

Mmhmm.

FRANCES smiles.

The music and rain get louder now until they begin to overwhelm the dialogue.

Maybe the lights begin to dim somehow, even though they're candles.

No keep going.

Oh no no I didn't mean to like – to play it down or anything. It's just the first time I've said that out loud.

Mmhmm yeah.

Really no. That's not what I meant at all.

JOEY plucks a tissue out of the box.

FRANCES's phone rings quietly. She answers it.

Yeah I know it's fucking bullshit. But thanks for playing along yeah? It actually does help.

Yeah exactly. I think it's about cutting yourself a bit of slack. You sound like a self-critical guy so I don't think you're gonna delude yourself.

The music and rain are so loud we can't hear them talking any more.

They just go on talking, eating, hunched round the tiny table.

Together.

Maybe there's a sudden blinding white light.

Or maybe we just listen to the song in the darkness.

The End.

A Nick Hern Book

You Stupid Darkness! first published in Great Britain in 2019 as a paperback original by Nick Hern Books Limited, The Glasshouse, 49a Goldhawk Road, London W12 8QP, in association with Paines Plough

Reprinted with revisions 2020

You Stupid Darkness! copyright © 2019, 2020 Sam Steiner

Sam Steiner has asserted his moral right to be identified as the author of this work

Cover design by Michael Windsor-Ungureanu, Thread Design
Image copyright © Cecilia Wessels

Designed and typeset by Nick Hern Books, London
Printed in the UK by Mimeo Ltd, Huntingdon, Cambridgeshire PE29 6XX

A CIP catalogue record for this book is available from the British Library

ISBN 978 1 84842 832 4

Woodland
CARBON

www.nickhernbooks.co.uk

 facebook.com/nickhernbooks

twitter.com/nickhernbooks